WAKING A SLEEPING GIANT

Theodore F. Kouba

VANTAGE PRESS
New York / Atlanta
Los Angeles / Chicago

With love and gratitude
to Marie Love Kouba,
who edited the manuscript

FIRST EDITION

All rights reserved, including the right of
reproduction in whole or in part in any form.

Copyright © 1987 by Theodore F. Kouba

Published by Vantage Press, Inc.
516 West 34th Street, New York, New York 10001

Manufactured in the United States of America
ISBN: 0-533-07267-0

Library of Congress Catalog Card No.: 86-90342

Contents

Preface   v

I. Destination Unknown   1
II. Challenging a Trackless Land   11
III. Uninvited Guests   25
IV. Nothing but Prairie and Sky   38
V. The Day Black Hawk Saw Red   61
VI. How a Chief Is Made   83
VII. Sitting Bull Wins the Big One   108
VIII. Mystery of the Indian Mounds   137
IX. Echoes of a Patriot   148
X. Contributions to Our Civilization   154
Epilogue   171

Appendixes
Appendix A. Finding Indian Relics Today   175
Appendix B. Identifying Stone Indian Artifacts   181
Bibliography   187

Preface

A band of Asian nomads seeking wildlife food unknowingly wandered over a recently exposed land bridge into a seemingly forgotten country. There they awakened a slumbering giant—the North American continent. What a strikingly different world!

No human footprints could be found inasmuch as no humans before set foot on the land. Winters were cruelly cold, summers unpredictably cool. Even worse, and unknown to the nomads at the time, an irresistible ice mountain lay heavily on vast portions of the continent. Still, under such horrendous conditions (circa twenty-five thousand years ago), these Asian nomads created a surprisingly sophisticated culture that forever belies their modern image as bloodthirsty savages. Gradually they transformed the Americas into a startlingly distinctive world.

At the beginning a single band set foot on the forbidding land. Threading its way along a mysterious route, the persevering primates, and later their progeny, suffered hardships beyond compare, plodding over ice fields that seemingly extended forever. After centuries, and pushing onward several hundred miles through the ice mountain, a more livable climate was discovered. Gradually a cultural richness surfaced. Still, the environment round about remained as fresh as an original thought. Few passages of history portray so bright a pattern of family togetherness, impassioned heroism, and disciplined bravery as demonstrated by these aboriginals whom modern white man mistakenly named Indians.

So let us pursue these testy Asian nomads—the first humans to set their moccasined feet on this North American continent. Somewhere, sometime, was the discovery of fire, a manifestation distinguishing man from beast. And the nomads took to mastering the physical world—first with stone-tipped spears, then with bow and arrow, though discreetly destroying none of it. Along the way they learned to use fire to cook food and to warm their bodies. And on and on it went!

After thousands of years, Europeans arrived. They found the land inhabited by these aboriginals who, though differing one tribe from another in some respects, held many comparable physical features and mental temperaments. Still, each tribe was fiercely individualistic. Quite strangely, they had light yellow or red-brown skin, eye pupils distinctly black, hair straight, black, and coarse, and facial and body hair uncommonly sparse.

To these white-skinned newcomers, a reservoir of intriguing questions surfaced. Who were these North American people, from where did they come, and what route had they taken? Unto this day the mystery of these ancient forerunners grips the interest of every inquiring mind. With each of their passing generations, death stole and lost forever countless secrets. When did they reach this continent, and what happened after their arrival? The writer hopes this story will unfold to the reader like the very pages of this book.

Surely American Indians are an intriguing race, differing greatly from one locale to the next. But, too often Caucasians labeled Indians as a group, a mob of murdering warriors, entirely overlooking the many instances in which they welcomed white man and considered him a trusted friend. And the character and loyalty of the Indian surely cannot be too severely questioned—wasn't he loyal first to his family and tribe? Even a songbird may fight to defend its young and its nest!

So, as the Indians were being pushed back from the land sacred to them, misunderstandings with whites arose. Indians of the prairies and plains, for instance, rightly felt they were being forcefully removed from their food, the bison, from their ancient tribal lands, and from their very homes. They saw their people dying from smallpox and other white man's diseases. They saw their customs fading into oblivion and bison herds disappearing before the onward march of white man. This thrust against their way of life was unpredictably foreign. All too suddenly whites began settling here, there, and everywhere—no place left for the Indian to roam free, no place to live. Soldiers—those with powerful "sticks" that spit thunder and lightning—began moving from point to point. All this whiteman aggressiveness changed the Indian's way of life. It also changed him!

So let us delve into the mysterious life of these nomads—not just their warfare, although bloodshed further accelerated the struggle, but the irascible situations that led to the wars and, more particularly, the very lives of Indians before white man. Surely this subject carries profuse excitement beyond the ordinary.

The Indian's philosophy of life in those early days is a storybook itself. To him the universe was a sounding board of every emotion that thrilled his being. He found in its phenomena the answer to his everyday life. He listened to the voice of nature. He said he belonged to the land and did not regard the land as a commodity belonging to him. To the prehistoric Indian, signs were symbolic. An excited bird darting across the trail by sudden impulse, an abrupt change in the wind, sharp lightning strikes followed by heavy thunder—all these signals and others challenged his deepest thoughts.

So if one follows the trail of these Asian nomads who unwittingly discovered this North American continent thousands of years ago, one can pause and reflect on how these people lived happily on the land for time unknown, keeping its air fresh, water pure, and forests and wildlife healthy. Not too strangely, they have almost been forgotten, which reminds us once again that the present, whenever it may be, soon melts into oblivion.

Waking a Sleeping Giant was written for the reader to relive the melodramatic narrative of North America's first immigrants. The book is a penetrating rhetoric of historic accounts reconstructed by anthropologists, archaeologists, and others who are recapturing the life of ancient times and includes subtle, discrete details previously not publicly disclosed. Scattered bits of information from diverse sources were painstakingly interpreted by the author, in an attempt to achieve a lifelike facsimile of primeval North America.

If this book, based upon rare and exciting footprints of the past, can carry the reader into an unpretentious world of long ago, the terrestrial arena of the Indians' happy hunting ground can be rediscovered.

I
Destination Unknown

On a date as mysterious as the people themselves, a courageous nomad Ice Age hunter clan unknowingly discovered a slumbering giant. Predators supreme, they set foot on an unnamed land countless millennia ago. Preying on huge creatures and hunting with infinite efficiency, the incomparable predators virtually exterminated beasts at each improvised camp and were forced onward. And they arrived at seemingly the worst time, when the deep-freeze of the Ice Age gripped the planet and lay heavily on the North American continent. What a secretive New World to reconnoiter!

Success of these hunters extraordinary was geared to ingenious weapons and predator techniques. Long before the bow and arrow was invented here, lengthy wooden shafts, tipped with razor-sharp stone spearheads that cut like our fine-honed steel scalpels, were used. Plunged deep in arteries and vital organs, these weapons drained life from the huge beasts.

Seldom in the annals of history have primitive people fought adversity so savagely. But let us zoom back into the awesome Ice Age, when the top half of North America groaned under gigantic glacial transformations.

The people came! Searching the mysterious beyond, they ventured onto a land never before seen by man. And they came—not from the south or east or west, but, of all places, from the north. Who were these people who discovered North America? Not Norsemen in A.D. 1006, as written in a Norse saga, nor Christopher Columbus in 1492. Nomads from northern Asia they were, exploring this new continent thousands of years before Columbus was born. Crediting Columbus with discovery of America is pure fabrication, and placing this fairy tale in our history books mixes fiction and fact.

Somewhat strangely, these predator nomads came not by way

ANCIENT MAN'S MIGRATION ROUTE TO NORTH AMERICA?

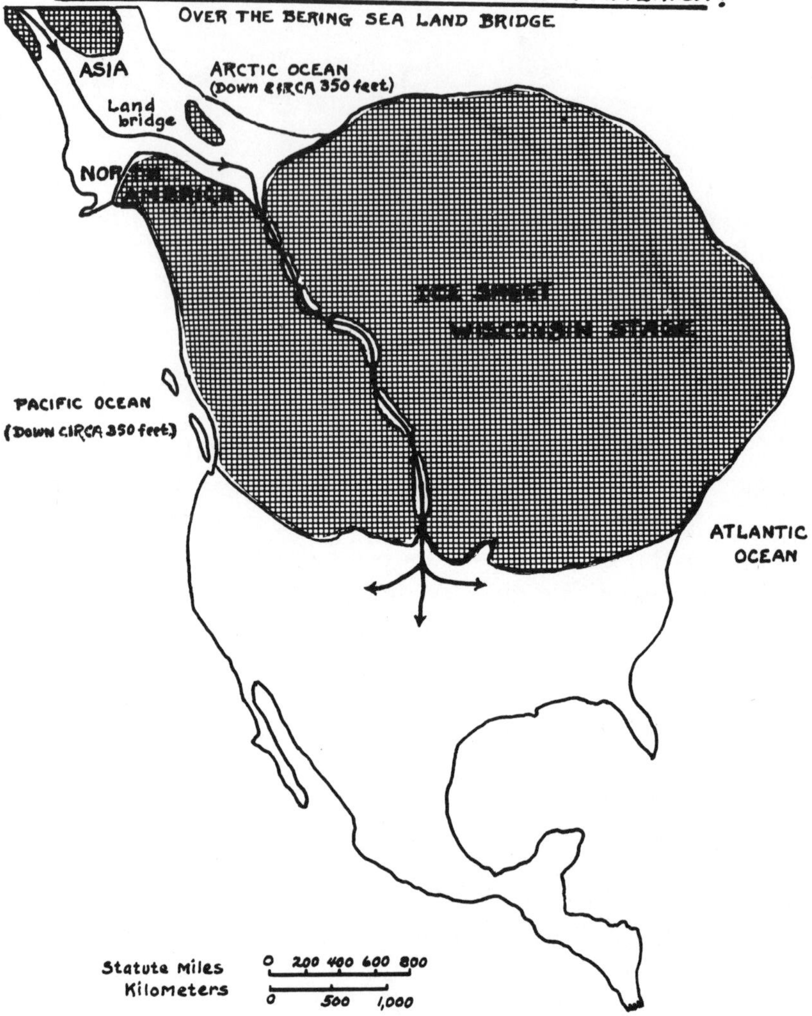

of the Aleutian Islands but, of all things, by way of the Bering Strait land bridge, submerged today, while following grazing herds and giant beasts that claimed the New World as their own. Alive with creatures and plants tuned to its harsh climate, these human newcomers arrived. Due to an avalanche of insoluble problems, the first band lost the fierce struggle and disappeared from the scene. Years later, others came. They too lost! Eventually poetic justice prevailed; a single band survived and its progeny moved onward. At long last the invasion barrier to North America was broken!

And the people came. Yes, criers of doom were among them, but those who prevailed shouted good tidings. When did they set foot on North America? Sometime during the period of the Wisconsin stage of the great Ice Age, a phenomenon of earthshaking drama. Over a mile thick at its center in the Hudson Bay region of Canada, the ice mountain tapered off at its distant edges. Covering most of Canada, the ice titan stretched southward into today's United States. Down as far as Philadelphia the ice moved: over Ohio, Indiana, Illinois, and Iowa; blanketing most of the Dakotas, covering the Great Lakes states, but for reasons known only to itself, it missed terrain in southwest Wisconsin, northwest Illinois, northeast Iowa, and southeast Minnesota called the Driftless Area. Born about ninety thousand years ago, this Wisconsin stage of the Ice Age was the last of four periods, covering roughly a million years. Moving over the land, the ice mass leveled the countryside.

Cautiously advancing onto the tip of North America, following grazing herds of that time, the first nomad band arrived. Alaska, through which the adventurous people wandered, was largely glacier-free except for mountain ranges. So here in the little-known past that covers centuries but passes like a thought today, the American continent first felt the tread of human feet and heard the voice of man.

The bands of nomads moved onward! They came when the glacial mountain drank much of the sea, lowering the oceans some three hundred feet and uncovering between Asia and North America a Bering Sea land bridge. The Little and Big Diomede islands of today were high points above the bleak grass and shrub landscape.

Who were these people? Mongoloid they were—mixed races from Asia. Unaccountably, none carried the extreme Mongoloidal features such as the eye fold. Yellow-brown skin, straight, coarse black hair they had—with facial and body hair uncommonly sparse. Eye pupils were dark, eyes set far apart, with cheekbones prominent. Noses, typically Mongolian, oftentimes were beaked—having a width midway between the thin nose of whites and thick nose of blacks.

Why the Ice Age at this particular time? And what set it in motion—lowering the oceans of the world and exposing the Bering Sea land bridge? Volcanic eruptions that flung tiny particles of debris high into the stratosphere, eliminating much sunshine from the earth, may have triggered it. But views differ. And why did the climate grow cold and wet, generating the glacier to form and grow and move, and why did it warm centuries later, forcing the gigantic ice mass covering a colossal area of the United States and Canada eventually to melt?

Scientists conclude that ice caps develop during periods of uncommonly heavy rains and snows rather than during centuries of unbelievable cold. Cold, yes, but mild winters are most conducive to frequent and heavy snowfalls, and the snow simply falls faster than it melts during summers. This circumstance initiated the Wisconsin stage of the great Ice Age, and like any glacial ice sheet, it was continually in slow motion. As snow fell on the ice surface, it was compressed into solid ice when additional layers of snow piled on top. Thus the ice moved sluggishly but steadily downward and outward to its distant edges. Then over eons of time a warmer period arrived—the ice slowly melted, and the seas gradually rose to their normal levels. Once again the Bering Sea land bridge was swallowed by the oceans. But this is getting ahead of the story.

So let us return to the land bridge! What else happened when the Bering Strait bridge surfaced? An astounding change shaped the regional climate. The bridge blocked the cold water of the Arctic Ocean from moving into the neighboring Pacific Ocean. From the opposite direction the comparatively warm Pacific water and air moving northward tempered the climate of the land between. Though the bridge was virtually glacier-free, still it was no sunshine paradise—the frigid Arctic bordering on one side and the Wisconsin ice cap at varying distances to the east and south. Yet a few hardy plants adjusted to the rigorous climate, driving roots into the stubborn soil. Small patches of green reached for the sky. Dangerous beasts walked the land, including the lion-sized cat that competed with man for big game. The caribou, musk ox, native small horse, and other wildlife provided meat for hunters during the early centuries. Strangely, the horse went north, crossed the bridge to Asia, and eventually disappeared from North America. Efficiency of the human predators also may have been too much! But Europeans in the sixteenth century A.D. introduced their much larger horse to the Americas.

The nomads came! Wandering over the land bridge, naively they moved through Alaska. But this was only the beginning! An avalanche of problems struck the leading band. Lost in the emptiness of the vast continent, these wanderers, plagued with a ferocity seldom shown by man, journeyed over the windswept land. Ahead the earth stretched to the sky. Stark stillness frightened them as they listened to the echoes of reality, and unknown to those who survived this demanding trudge was the fact that no human foot had touched the land since creation.

When early morning's sun yawned across the unknown land, the nomads pulled on their fur-lined boots as they slept in skins covering their bodies. A dog sniffed at the base of a dwarfed tree and lazily lifted a leg. Erelong the sun was wide awake, showing a bloody red, perhaps a portent of events to come.

With faces as weathered as choice apples left too long in the hot sun, the nomads willingly wagered their very lives, for living in so hostile an environment is one of the greatest skills known to man. Comforts? Only in their dreams! And the only music they could hear were sounds of silence. Even the weather at times turned against the floundering band, changing from one of beauty to an ugly overpowering force. Clouds that did not mind their manners spit out hail and rain. Snowflakes tumbled downward, and fog, like prison walls, fenced in the struggling few. Pain and suffering—constant companions—shaped their character. Nothing surely, except huge beasts, felt at home in this desolate land that had no end.

The nomads moved on, generation after generation. But then, a herculean task confronted them. Reaching a precipitous rise where the ice mass of the giant glacier loomed, their movement east, west, and south seemed blocked. As they cautiously probed here and there, clearly in search of direction, a narrow ice-free corridor provided an uncertain pathway south. This unique passage through the towering ice cap apparently existed between eighteen and twenty-eight thousand years ago, when the Cordilleran (Rocky Mountain) and the Laurentian (Eastern North America) glacial lobes did not quite meet. This sometimes ice-free corridor snaked in a generally southern direction—up the Yukon Valley, then up the Mackenzie River Valley past Great Bear Lake, then to Reindeer Lake, Lake Athabaska, and Lake Winnepeg, into North Dakota and Minnesota. Other partial routes may have been available also.

When food grew scarce, the foremost band, not knowing others were following, struggled on, usually southward. Those who survived always discovered a green valley in the distance where wildlife was abundant. And so it went!

But as far as these people knew, there was no Ice Age. Hadn't the mountains of ice always been there generation after generation? To them the ice cliffs were as permanent as the Antarctic Ice Cap is to us today. And there is no valid reason to assume that the people were consciously migrating. They moved on as food conditions dictated, taking any route open to them, and no special instinct drove them southward. Hadn't their Asian ancestors centuries earlier traveled northward—finally reaching the Bering Strait land bridge?

When did these ancient people reach North America? Only a century ago it was virtually irreligious to affirm that primitive society existed here more than six thousand years ago. But this has undergone a radical change in the lifetime of two or three generations of archaeologists. Recent evidence suggests that prehistoric people arrived circa twenty-five thousand years ago, perhaps earlier. But no one is sure. Further corroboration continues to push the discovery date farther back. A few distiguished men of science theorize that man came to North America earlier. Dr. Louis S. B. Leakey believes that people have been on this continent more than fifty thousand years. So the time of ancient man's entry here is as uncertain as the reconstruction of a dream, although there is certainty that man arrived many thousands of years ago. And there is almost unanimity of agreememt that the people were Asians—not Caucasians. When Columbus, a Caucasian, reached these shores, he named the natives Indians, thinking he landed in India, and the name remains to this day! So now we have Indians of America and Indians of India, with no known blood relationship between the two races.

But back to ancient man! Let no one as much as whisper that this human who survived the bedeviled elements of the time was an ineffective hunter. From the distant past he was a hunter—not an ordinary hunter albeit, but perhaps the most skillful predator the world has known. He was supremely successful even without all the natural armaments of beasts—no fangs to tear flesh, no tusks, no cat quickness, no eyes to see through darkness, no protective coat of thick hide or fur. Endowed with an inventive brain, early man simply outthought the beasts he hunted. Stone weapons he flaked and propelled with astounding accuracy served him more effectively than any body armor he lacked. Over time, ancient man of America became the dominant predator and carnivore of the animal kingdom.

Few in number, the nomads moved on—men, women, children, struggling along a trail of no return. Suffer they did, though not necessarily in silence. A language they had—enough words to communicate and hand signs. Fire they knew, even perhaps how to make it, yet lightning may have been their chief fire source. In the beginning, nomads who used fire incautiously surely set their huts or dry grass nearby alight or the forest ablaze before they learned to control and use fire judiciously. Paying dearly in this awkward manner, eventually they discovered how to use the flame to warm their bodies, to cook food, and to protect themselves from wild beasts.

And what have we named these aboriginal upstarts—the first humans to tread the North American soil? Paleo-Indians—emphasis on ancient, primitive. Possessing a tenacious determination, these comparatively short, muscular nomads painfully adjusted to a conglomeration of unprecedented dilemmas. Using bone, horn, and stone they developed a toolmaking skill approximating their Stone Age contemporaries unknown to them in Europe, and to make their hunting weapon more useful and deadly, they invented the atlatl throwing-stick, a contraption that noticeably increased a spear's velocity. With the throwing-stick, the spear could better penetrate the thick, tough hide of prehistoric mammals and imbed itself in their vital organs.

But then, as now, time moved on. Centuries passed. Then, incredibly, about twelve thousand years ago in our North America a new phenomenon struck. The climate turned warmer and drier.

And the ice-cap mountain began to melt and recede. This climatic eruption sparked a paramount change in the life of ancient man here. Forced to adjust, he did so, exceeding his own presumptions.

Large beasts of the Ice Age, like the mastodon and mammoth, did not adapt to the warmer temperatures. To survive, they followed for centuries plants growing in the cool climate of the receding glacier, but gradually these huge mammals became extinct. Could it be they turned sterile from the change of environment, as many zoo animals do? The hunters continued to follow the beast, but then the warmer climate southward from the glacial ice appealed to these ancient people and more of them chose to live where the weather was less debilitating. And the large beasts continued to follow the glacier, with smaller game taking their place. Though still a hunter supreme, ancient man did not wander far from camp. When he learned that the spear, effective against huge Ice Age creatures, was not the right weapon for the smaller, quicker animals, he refined his hunting instruments and invented a new contrivance, the bow and arrow. With a sharper, smaller stone point, cleverly made, securely fastened to the tip of a thin, round wooden shaft, he propelled this razor-sharp, stone-tipped shaft from a bow with speed and force. The bow ancient man carried was richly decorated with ornamental patterns fashioned from plant dyes, symbolizing the history of his particular clan, as many of these mortals were admirable primitive artists. Scientists of our day have discovered preserved in dry-climate caves, bone, tusk, and wooden tools and weapons shaped and decorated by these early people. The artifacts found reveal an intriguing story of a long-ago civilization.

How is the age of this ancient civilization determined? Not by guess—far be it! Scientists first obtained the age of archaeological remains using dendrochronology (the science of tree rings). Annual rings of the ancient wooden substance are compared with those of a growing tree, age known. From these data it was determined during the thirteenth century that the population of the pueblo world of our southwest began to shrink markedly, and it was tree rings that tattletaled the long and murderous drought, a period of twenty-three virtually rainless years from A.D. 1276 through A.D. 1299.

The tree-ring system provides a bank of knowledge on environment and time and is used as a bridge to link, within tree-age

Drawing by Charles Schwartz.

The caribou—one animal that served as a source of food during early centuries.

limitations, the present with the historic past. A tree is a faithful timekeeper. Strangely, despite small size, the bristlecone pine of our Southwest is the oldest timekeeper known, reaching six thousand years. Scientists sometimes use tree-ring samples to correct radiocarbon dates. It was in the late 1940s that radiocarbon dating surfaced. By using charcoal from early man's campfires or wood, bone, horn, or textiles these early people used, an item's approximate age is calculated. This method is called Carbon 14 or radiocarbon dating. These substance materials are tested in a laboratory to compute the residue of a radioactive isotope of carbon, designated as Carbon 14.

Carbon 14 is present in most living organisms, and when these no longer are alive, it disintegrates in fixed proportion from the substance. This method can effectively measure up to forty thousand years. A margin of error occurs, although no more than a few hundred years in several thousands.

More recently, however, a new dating technique was developed, based on changes that evolve in the amino acid of bone protein after death. This method can reach appreciably farther into the past than radiocarbon dating can. By these methods cited, and by other skillful determinations, man's presence in America has been pushed back dramatically.

Baptized by scientific "fire," scholars agree man came to North America from Asia. But the date he arrived is a profound mystery. So did he arrive twenty-five thousand years ago, more or less, as many scientists contend, or as far back as fifty thousand years ago, a date a few scholars favor? That he shaped raw stone into spear points, attached these to ends of wood or bone shafts, and thus devised weapons that gave him a distinct advantage over wild beasts of the land is noncontroversial. It is these stone artifacts and the organic substances he shaped and left behind at many locations in North America that prove ancient man lived here in an era long before recorded history.

II

Challenging a Trackless Land

Secreted between mountains of ice in valleys harboring pockets of green vegetation, the invading nomad bands lived and died. Not consciously migrating, they threaded their way through the hostile environment. Food they pursued ferociously—surely as necessary as the air they breathed—and over centuries one nomad band snaked its way through the glacial ice cap. Others eventually triumphed. Once free of the ice mountain, southward, westward, and eastward they trekked. Toward Mexico of today a few bands wandered. Others skirted the southern edge of the glacier—moving eastward toward today's Mississippi River, the Great Lakes, and beyond. Tundra[1] for unknown distances extended from the ice mountains. Farther still was a forest of spruce and fir, tree species favoring cool temperatures. In such an environment the surviving nomads hunted the huge, powerful beasts of that era.

Water in the Great Lakes, higher then than now, drained southward into the Mississippi River. But a few thousand years later, when the glacier retrogressed farther north, the water course changed direction, draining eastward into the Atlantic Ocean through the St. Lawrence River, and so it does unto this day.

But back to these superb huntsmen who harassed the giant creatures following the snail's-pace ice cap! Extraordinary hunters, yes, but how could a half-dozen men with primitive weapons subdue such phenomenally powerful mammals as the mastodon and giant bison? Only one way. By outthinking the brawny beasts! Cleverly, Ice Age men improvised ways to approach the mammals without stampeding them, as these beasts had never seen a human being. Also, at new locations, wildlife was so prevalent the meat supply

---

[1] Plains covered with a thick matting of dwarfed vegetation, largely shrubs and stunted trees.

Paleo-Indians kill young mastodon for food. Mother attacks.
TFK

was essentially unlimited. With mastodon the target, a young beast with meat tender and flavorsome was selected—not an old creature with flesh tough and sinewy. And death of a mastodon surely was not instantaneous. Stone-tipped spears hurled into its body at key positions pierced the mastodon's arteries and vital organs. As the beast was fighting furiously, the vibrating wooden shafts kept the blood flowing! Through heavy blood loss the beast was unable to keep with the herd—then the pursuing hunters rushed in with stones and clubs, dispatching the creature, or they waited nearby for its eventual death.

And how did these new immigrants hunt the prehistoric bison as distinguished from the smaller bison of our day? Ice Age men, dressed in wolfskins, crawled on hands and knees and hid at waterholes. Wolves commonly followed bison herds; thus the wolfskin covering, and the then unrecognized scent of humans, attracted no special attention. Hunters also may have howled like wolves to complete the deception.

Clearly, these ancient hunters with a ferocity rarely shown by man, had admirable courage, even a degree of recklessness, to pit their small but muscular bodies against the giant beasts. Although their diet was primarily meat, this was augmented by seeds and fruits in season. One can say that animals and plants supplied almost everything—food, shelter, clothing, and utensils—all except stone, which they found along the way and flaked for weapons.

Take the encounter eight thousand years ago—ages before white man brought the modern horse to America. This hunting party, using its own primitive methods, attacked a herd of bison not far from today's Denver, Colorado. Afoot these hunters stampeded the herd, driving the bison headlong into an arroyo 170 feet deep. Then they butchered the animals on the spot. Scientists from the University of Colorado museum excavated the site and recorded the hunt in infinite detail. So well reserved were the bison bones, it was determined with some degree of certainty the date the hunt occurred, the route of the drive, the organized manner of butchering their quarry, and the choice morsels eaten at the location.

One of the first and probably *the* first reliable report of a stone artifact being found with an American mastodon occurred in 1897. The skeleton, found by small sons of a farmer near Boaz in Richland County, Wisconsin, was about nine thousand years old. Paleo-Indian

Bison hunting before the horse was introduced to America.

hunters presumably killed the beast, and a quartzite Folsom spear point was found with the skeleton. The fluted point was chipped from quartzite the hunters probably quarried at Silver Mound,[1] eighty miles north in today's Jackson County. Residuum of this mastodon now is displayed at the University of Wisconsin–Madison Geology Museum. Left leg bones of the huge beast are natural, the right replicas. Is it possible it died lying on the left side with its body covering those legs, then the Paleo-Indian attackers severed and took the free right legs with them for food?

In the 1970s, researchers at Washington State University uncovered direct evidence that mastodons were hunted by humans eleven to fourteen thousand years ago in the state of Washington. Found was a broken rib with a spearhead extending three-quarters of an inch therefrom. Of special interest also, Soviet scientists in eastern Siberia excavated a giant block of ice containing a perfectly preserved baby mammoth about six months old with reddish hair, big feet, and small ears.

What about this giant mastodon which stood nine feet high at the shoulder and compared strikingly to its distant relative, the elephant of our day? What do we know about the life of this gro-

---

[1] Charles E. Brown, Silver Mound (47-Ja-21), *Prehistoric Quarrying at Silver Mound*, Manuscript Collection, Archives Division, State Historical Society, Madison, Wisconsin.

Skeleton of mastodon uncovered near Boaz, Wisconsin, in 1897.

Courtesy of the Geology Museum of the University of Wisconsin, Madison, Wisconsin

tesque creature, which disappeared from the North American scene long ago? Much! The mammal has been studied by scholars in many states, among them Dr. Warren L. Wittry, who researched the creature in Michigan. Through radiocarbon dating it was learned that Indians in that state hunted the mastodon as early as twelve thousand years ago and that it did not become extinct until about 4,000 B.C. Thus ancient man and the beast lived together in Michigan, and apparently other states with comparable conditions, for six thousand years. And did Indians hunt mastodon purely for sport? It was learned the mammal was hunted primarily for food.

Surprisingly over a hundred mastodons have come to light in Michigan alone, mostly bone and teeth accidentally discovered by men with machines. But Wittry studied a mastodon skeleton uncovered by the Cranbrook Institute of Science in Lapeer county in 1965 and 1966 in detail. Most ribs had been cut from the vertebrae by man with a cutting tool, presumably a stone knife, with marks showing on the edges of joints. Cutting tools also were used to saw ligaments when one bone was pried from another. Twenty feet from its proper position on the skeleton, the skull lay with three large pieces near the left hind leg. The skull fragments apparently had been removed to reach the brain, which the hunters considered choice. Cutting marks also were visible where the skull had been pried from the vertebra.

Archaeology in America has had many priceless moments, but one of its brightest stars was a discovery in 1926 near Folsom, New Mexico. Found was a stone spearhead embedded between two Ice Age bison ribs. Here, along with other disclosures, was further uncontested proof that man had been in North America during the time of Ice Age mammals. Named Folsom for the village, this point type is the next thing to perfection.

Thin, shaped like a handmade paper dart, exquisitely flaked, a Folsom point has a flute running up one or both sides almost to the tip, permitting it to be firmly lashed into the cleft end of a wooden or bone shaft. Strong-armed Paleo-Indians drove it through the thick, tough hide of a beast, penetrating selected arteries and vital organs. But Folsom Man flaked other stone artifacts also, as end and side scrapers—knives, stoneheads, perforators, and gravers, to name a few. This ancient man lived roughly six to twelve thousand years ago, with isolated clans presumably living here at a much earlier date, not in New Mexico only, as Folsom spear points have been found at various locations of the United States, Canada, and Mexico. The author found Folsom and related artifacts (including shaped round stones, either hand-held or attached to a handle) on the ground surface at a site in Dane County, Wisconsin. Through years of farm cultivation, the field lost the thin upper topsoil layers at infrequent locations. Thus artifacts of a long-gone civilization became visible.

But there were other Paleo-Indian people. Take Clovis man—now considered a civilization older than Folsom. It is believed these people lived in North America nine to fifteen thousand or more years ago. Clovis spearpoints are generally larger and thicker than Folsom and rarely as carefully flaked. Still, they usually have a flute on one or both sides, but seldom does it extend farther than halfway down the point. Clovis artifacts have been found and reported from locations in the United States and Canada and as far south as Panama, but, insofar as known, nowhere else in the world. Yet to this day they are rare finds. The late Dr. Robert E. Ritzenthaler, when curator of the Milwaukee Public Museum, released photographs of some of the author's Paleo-Indian artifacts and described them in the December 1966 and September 1967 issues of *The Wisconsin Archeologist,* calling the geographic location the Kouba Site.

A civilization in North America that some scientists consider older than Clovis is that of Sandia man. Deposits in caves located in the Sandia Mountains of New Mexico disclosed that Paleo-Indians may have lived in them as much as twenty-five thousand years ago and hunted animals, some that no longer exist. Bones of the prehistoric horse, camel, bison, mastodon, and mammoth were found, presumably debris from meals of ancient hunters who frequented the caves. During excavation of a site, two layers of Sandia man spearpoints were discovered at the bottom—below Folsom and Clovis. Their location below Clovis and Folsom lends credence to the belief that they are an older age, though this deduction has not been accepted by all archaeologists. But the fact that Dr. H. M. Wormington of the Denver Museum of Natural History—one of many who believe Sandia points are among the earliest man-made stone forms in America and may represent the original pattern from which later types were developed carries appreciable weight. Two types of Sandia points were found. Interestingly, the lower level spearheads were cruder and thicker than those above them. Like Clovis, some Sandia points have flutes extending partway down one or both sides. And about this flute! From whom did the Paleo-Indians learn the extremely difficult art of fluting? Most likely from their own ancestors!

Still, at first blush, little is known about our earliest Americans. At the original Folsom, Clovis, and Sandia sites and other camping places of these ancient hunters, no human bones were found, which seems astoundingly unnatural. Primitive people on other continents usually buried their dead or threw out the bones with camp refuse. Today, some authorities believe primitive people of America burned their dead during special ceremonies. Even if this were true, fragments or bits of charred bone should be found.

A few human skeletons of early man have been discovered, however. These principally date to when aboriginal man hunted ancient animals, as the skeleton found near Mexico City at the small village Tepexpan. Incarcerated in a layer of soil, it included mammoth skeletons. Unfortunately, no Folsom, Clovis, or Sandia spearheads were found with or near the skeletons. Nor were scrapers or other implements nearby to date the site.

Profound attention has been drawn to the Old Copper Culture people of the Great Lakes region, centered in Wisconsin. Until recently, it was believed these people who made weapons and ornaments from native copper lived at this location a mere 1,500 years ago. But later excavations set the date back to the period five to seven thousand years ago, an early age for shaping and using metal anywhere in the world.[1] Native copper, chiefly ingots found on the ground surface, although some mined, was pounded into useful and ornamental articles.

Excavations of gigantic importance continue. Take the Koster site. Being unearthed here is a civilization dating back perhaps to 7500 B.C., covering generation upon generation of prehistoric America. Named the Koster site for the farm owner, it lies in west-central Illinois near the confluence of the Illinois and Mississippi rivers. After several years of excavation, and more to follow, it may be the most data-productive excavation in the United States during this century.

---

[1] McKern, 1941; Quimby, 1952; Wittry and Ritzenthaler, 1956.

Koster is extraordinarily significant because it has what appears to be thirteen or more distinct periods of habitation, dating from about A.D. 1000 (Mississippi Period) at the top back to B.C. 7500 (Early Archaic Period) at the bottom. Of colossal magnitude was the discovery of rounded post holes indicating the presence of permanent homes as many as seven thousand years ago—far earlier than was thought existed in the prehistoric United States. Tree trunks as much as ten inches in diameter were cut for this purpose. Horizon 6 was occupied the longest and—can you fancy this?—for about one thousand years.

What made the many distinct layers of occupation possible? With the homes located beneath a limestone bluff, when the settlement moved, fine loam from the high land washed down over a period of time and covered the area. When another group of prehistoric people settled on the spot, they were unaware that previously abandoned settlements lay beneath—the earliest thirty-five feet below the present ground surface.

And what did these early Americans eat? Deer, swan, goose, duck, and fish, including freshwater mussels, were the primary food sources. Seeds and nuts were other significant foods. To everyone's surprise, it seems they drank a broth concocted from hickory and other nuts and ate at least two kinds of porridge—one from acorn flour, the other from seeds of marsh elder and pigweed.

Discovered at Horizon 1 (the period of about A.D. 1000) was extensive evidence of violence. Burial remains disclosed deaths of many persons from arrow and spear wounds. And why was warfare waged during this period? Perhaps due to a rapid population expansion—the fastest increase in the prehistory of the Illinois River valley. Food competition surely triggered the violence. No sign points to Koster inhabitants being annihilated. These early Americans quite possibly could be living at this location today if white people had not appeared and used the land for their own purposes.

A culture based on agriculture surfaced when pod corn, a primitive maize, was discovered in Bat Cave, New Mexico. Here maize grown by ancient man was radiocarbon-dated as being five to six thousand years old. And how did plant cultivation in the New World begin? Let us speculate that someplace in the distant past ancient people, while gathering wild seeds for food, found a plant with seeds or fleshy fruit far superior to those on other plants nearby. So what did they do? They returned to the choice plant year after year. Perhaps they encouraged its growth by digging around it or planted seeds from its stalks. Doing so, these people began the art of domestic cultivation. Though maize cultivation in America began early, scientists now believe that bean, squash, and gourd cultivation preceded maize.

A find of historic significance took place near Pelican Rapids, Minnesota, in 1931 where highway workmen uncovered a skeleton associated with two artifacts. Deposited in glacial silt about ten feet below the ground surface, the almost complete skeleton was studied not in situ. Yet the workmen who uncovered it applied reasonable care. Brought to the attention of A. E. Jenks of the University of Minnesota, the site was redug and bone fragments that fit parts of the skeleton were examined *in situ*.

Named Minnesota man at the time, the specimen proved to be a girl about fifteen who may have drowned in Lake Pelican, a glacial lake formed by the retreating Wisconsin glacier. Lying with vertebrae and ribs were an eight-inch-long antler dagger perforated at one end and a conch shell with two perforations. These apparently were suspended from a thong tied around the girl's neck or at the girdle. Surprisingly, the conch shell is common to the Gulf of Mexico and suggests contact with that distant region.

Although radiocarbon tests of the dagger were attempted, its carbon content ran so heavily to inorganic carbonate that no accurate date was possible. But mineralization to such a degree suggests antiquity. Controversy about the skeleton's age does exist, centering on whether it is the same age as the clay deposit or was placed there at a later date. Most students of the subject agree that Minnesota man is about ten thousand years old and lived in close proximity to the retreating glacier.

The murky death trap of prehistoric wildlife, La Brea tar pits, is as mysterious as illuminating. Located in Los Angeles's Hancock Park, the soil cavities into which petroleum seeped are being probed for ancient human and animal skeletons. When exposed to air, the petroleum mixture changes to asphalt, forming an extremely sticky tar. Pit edges become as hard as blacktop of our present-day roads, while their centers remain soft tar. When rain falls on the tar, the surfaces glisten like pools of water. Prehistoric animals that came to drink discovered too late that the "pools" were gummy death traps. They fell in and remain therein to this day.

What have scientists found in these tar pits? Skeletons of several extinct creatures of the Ice Age that fell into the pits ten to forty thousand year ago! Strangest perhaps are the bones of a modern-size horse with hoofs decidedly different from those on our present-day horses. Found in one pit in 1914 was the skull of a woman perhaps twenty-five years of age. Radiocarbon tests revealed that she fell into the pit about nine thousand years ago.

Discovered also were saw marks by primitive man made with a stone knife on "green" mammal bones. The bones radiocarbon-dated at fourteen thousand years. Equally significant was a pointed 9 1/2-inch long tooth, shaped like a sword, identified as belonging to the vicious sabertoothed cat of the Ice Age. This powerful short-tailed killer used its teeth as stabbing weapons to sever the arteries of its victims.

How about the Mongoloid bands that progressed southward into today's Mexico and Central and South America? Almost unbelievably over time the culture of these people developed into a civilization far superior to that of the more combative bands farther north. Of this peaceful southern group, the Maya (pronounced my-ah, a Spanish spelling) were supremely brilliant. It appears these people in some pursuits were the farthest advanced in the world during ancient times. When did the Maya culture prevail? History and archaeology, of course, begin at the same location, but archaeology takes off in the opposite direction and goes back in time. History being silent, archaeology necessarily provides the answer. It tells us the culture persisted from the third to the sixteenth century over an area of approximately 125,000 square miles (325,000 square kilometers) in portions of Yucatán, Guatamala, Belize, Honduras, and eastern Mexico, a territory roughly the size of Italy.

During the Maya Classic Age, the peak of this high-culture civilization persisted about six hundred years—almost as long as the entire life of the Roman Empire from Julius Caesar to Romulus Augustulus and which ran somewhat parallel in time. These early people persevered in this southern clime for time unknown; however, we are certain about some dates, as the Carbon 14 test at a Maya ceremonial center in Guatemala registering 1182 B.C. ($\pm$ 240).

Maya communities were primarily ceremonial centers, marketplaces, and government quarters, with temples and palaces built on terraces or pyramids. In addition to the great pyramids usually topped with temples, some centers contained aqueducts, bridges, stairways of stupendous size, structures with vapor baths, ceremonial public squares, and observation posts from which priests studied heavenly objects.

The common person lived in a thatched wooden hut and grew crops, including beans, squash, gourds, cattails for their roots, and maize. Growing crops suggests a sedentary life even in those ancient times; accordingly, Maya laborers were married to the soil and were scattered in timberland clearings. But the aggressive forest fought unyieldingly to recapture the small openings; thus growing crops was a continuous lifelong struggle.

Nature worship of the pre–Classic Age underwent multitudinous modifications, perhaps as early as the fourth century B.C., when astronomy, chronology, and hieroglyphic writing were introduced. Divinized heavenly bodies then had been added to the visionary gods of rain and maize. It must be said that while Mayan priests had acquired astounding knowledge of astronomical phenomena and a proficient concept of time, their own doctrines differed markedly from common myths of the ordinary people. So the priests alone continued studying and developed impressive architectural, calendrical, and mathematical accomplishments.

Even in those ancient times they comprised a precise written language—hieroglyphic ideographs, i.e., refined symbols representing words, as in Chinese writing. A few scholars today believe these symbols represent phonetic sounds, as used in our own alphabet. Overflowing with desire and striving for further knowledge, these progeny of Mongoloid nomads progressed on the educational trail. Inasmuch as Maya priests became expert at astronomy and acquired a sophisticated perception of time, their abstruse doctrines differed appreciably from the then popular myths. Incredibly, they developed two sensational calculations: positional numeration and the zero. Even today these are considered two of the greatest proficiencies of the human mind. Yet these achievements were no further advanced than their astronomy. The Maya calendar, improved over centuries by profound observations of sun, moon, planet Venus, and other heavenly bodies, developed through a system of twenty (fingers and toes counted instead of fingers only by our method) and by employing positional numbers and zero. Somewhat surprisingly, these two ideas were not conceived in Europe until ten centuries later.

No record relates the many centuries required for Mayan priests to calculate and refine their calendars and to finalize their written language. Not known also is whether Mayas acquired some phases from other people, such as the proto-Olmecs. If they had, something entirely uncertain at this time, it would be comparable to the ancient Greeks, who obtained some phases of their alphabet from the Phoenicians.

Without question, Maya calendrical computations over centuries followed a complex route. Calculated with amazing accuracy was the length of the solar year, as well as the synodical revolution of Venus. Furthermore, the priests predicted solar eclipses from their precise Venusian and lunar tables.

Maya calendars, though exceedingly accurate, were everything but easy to understand. *Tzolkin,* a 260-day sacred component of the year, was the simplest unit of the various day counts and was perhaps based on the period between autumn and spring. The other 105 days, plus a fraction, apparently represented a period committed to the planting and growing season. Days were marginally extended to acquire precise readings, which our present calendar partially includes during leap years. While scholars today attempt to unravel all intricacies of Maya calendric calculations—and they are indeed impressive—we have learned that their calendar in general use at the time was one ten-thousandth of a day per year more accurate than ours is today.

Somewhat strangely, social groups did not fraternize. Priests, sorcerers, hunters, fishermen, beekeepers, and others who were married to a productive vocation celebrated individually during religious get-togethers and feasts.

Metallurgy understandably was unknown among the Maya, as they had no hematite nearby from which metal could be made. Yet without iron and draft animals, except dogs perhaps, and with no wheel (though logs were expertly rolled to move objects), they achieved the highest civilization ancient America had ever known.

Even though we may think we know the Mayas, most of their life remains a profound mystery. Time for them has stopped, while for us it has moved on. Their sculptured figures on temples illuminate a few messages, yet they do not speak. Furthermore, during the collapse of the classic phase of their civilization, initiated presumably during peasant revolts, the incomparable cities Uxmal and Chichén-Itzá were sacked and abandoned; thus meaningful materials were largely destroyed. A more militaristic group, Itzá, overpowered the cultured Maya (circa 1000 A.D.) and instilled different doctrines and beliefs. Introduced also were central-Mexico Toltec customs of human sacrifice and oppressive militarism. Built were grandiose militant Toltec monuments such as the Temple of Warriors. Foreign gods replaced Mayan gods. This renaissance, lasting about two centuries, led to burdensome hegemony and was followed by fierce, continuous warfare.

The Maya civilization, so progressive, so brilliant, so precise, which followed a peaceful path of no return, has given more to the world than they knew. Their superb culture, tortured by the Itzá, hit rock bottom with the Spanish conquest in A.D. 1541.

III

Uninvited Guests

Many centuries passed in the northland also. Incomprehensible secrets of the warlike nomads near the glacial mountain remain untold. When the south face of the ice barrier eventually receded, the environment round about became more livable. Population increased, triggering open conflicts for choice locations. Over time, weaker clans united for self-defense while others joined forces to achieve superior offensive manpower. Tribes eventually formed. Forceful leaders were chosen.

Indians of the Northeast, for instance, fashioned the illustrious league of the Iroquois, joining five tribes—Mohawk, Cayuga, Onondaga, Oneida, and Seneca. Beginning about A.D. 1500, this league became the indomitable ruler of the spacious territory westward from Maine to Lake Michigan and southward to the Cumberland River in Tennessee. During the next two hundred years they were the domineering force neighboring tribes feared.

But then things changed! Uninvited guests came to America, those strange-looking people with white skin. Norsemen arrived early and either decided not to stay or were driven away. Spaniards came in the fifteenth and sixteenth centuries and left an unenviable record. Then Frenchmen came to capture the lush fur trade, primarily beaver. By 1608, when they founded Quebec, French fur traders had been active thereabouts for years. Other Europeans arrived—Dutch and English. The English?

First, Englishmen landed midway down the east coast, where the powerful Algonkian tribe ruled supreme. In 1607 three ships were sent to America to develop trade with the enigmatic people of the New World. Sailing into Chesapeake bay and settling in the gloom and silence of a dark virgin forest, Indian natives watched the pale-skinned trespassers' every move. The Englishmen were not military men. Neither were they adventurers. They were traders, actually men of means, but about as qualified to challenge the wilderness as the ill-fated *Titanic* was three centuries later to defy icebergs. Thus their careers in the New World were marked by great desire but little ability. One miscalculation surrendered to another. It was a tasteless life. With some misgiving they went about their business, erecting a crude village on the banks of a picturesque river they named James after their king, James I. The settlement they called Jamestown. They had a shortage of everything but inefficiency and floundered in a mudhole of problems. All would have perished had it not been for a kind thirteen-year-old Indian girl, Princess Pocahontas, who saved the life of the prestigious captain of this first permanent English settlement in North America—Capt. John Smith.

Leader of the dominant Algonkian tribe, Chief Powhatan, was a weird character—rude, sullen, suspicious. But then, strangely, his personality changed like sunshine breaking through a dark cloud when presented with a baby daughter of such cheerful nature she was given a name meaning "beautiful" and "playful." The name? Pocahontas—Princess Pocahontas!

For miles unknown, Chief Powhatan ruled the people of the vast forest around Jamestown. Smaller tribes over this vast area joined his Algonkians or their trail of no return ended abruptly. Powhatan ruled thirty tribes, boasting two hundred villages. Each tribe had a chief with some degree of independence, but who was still subservient to Powhatan. So the supreme power of this Algonkian confederacy was vested solely in the dynamic leader, Chief Powhatan, who lived in a spacious village at the falls of James River, where Richmond, Virginia, is located today.

These were difficult times for the people of Jamestown. Yet the Indians were causing them no trouble. It seems that both whites and Indians were following a course of peaceful coexistence. But Chief Powhatan knew the score. He put the problem on the backburner or, in Algonkian terms, on the back campfire. Settlers of Jamestown were dying by the dozens. He knew the settlement would not last. After all, these were the only white-skinned people in the world, insofar as he knew. Of the first 900 colonists who came in the period 1607 to 1609, mostly men, only 150 discouraged and physically weakened individuals remained alive in 1610. Powhatan easily could have exterminated them or let them starve. He did neither!

Princess Pocahontas was the apple of her father's eyes. She was as pretty and kind as her father was ruthless and remorseless. Her warmth and intelligence made him extremely fond of her, realizing that love toward others was a quality he himself lacked. She played hard, but was equally effervescent in pursuit of knowledge. She spent much time with her mother, watching her make pots from clay and mats from reeds. She saw her mother use a sharp edge of flint to cut tanned deerskin into pieces then fashion them into clothing, and Pocahontas listened intently while her mother told her about the great spirit the tribe worshiped and the benefits they derived in the form of sun, rain, trees, and animals. She explained that one must be kind to fully receive these many blessings. There was just no end to all her mother knew.

Then she told Pocahontas that the Algonkians, after every autumn harvest, thanked the great Spirit. "We call the day Harvest day," she confided. So when the settlers of Jamestown learned of the Indian Harvest day, they liked the idea. Thus after a bountiful harvest, among cidery scents from gnarled hawthorn trees, Pilgrims in America celebrated white man's first Thanksgiving feast and prayer in 1621. Thanksgiving Day has been extolled by Americans since.

But back again to 1607, when suddenly these strange white-skinned people who called themselves Englishmen came. They seemed as pale as a sick Indian to Pocahontas, who wondered why they were not a healthy brown. They came in the largest boats she had ever seen, each pushed by a huge sail. They built a settlement they called Jamestown on land dominated by her tribe. She thought it was wrong that they did not ask permission of her father to build there. They acted like it was their land, and they didn't care if they angered her father, even though he was so powerful everyone trembled when he frowned.

At Jamestown the forest echoed from ringing axes, from trees falling, from hammers pounding, and from the dull thud of spades digging holes in which to set poles for the protecting palisade. With no advance warning, two tall muscular Indians appeared. They were men of dignity with headdresses of colorful turkey feathers. Communication between the two groups was difficult, but it was learned that the two Indians were special messengers from the chief of a nearby village and that in a few days their leader would come to visit. This pleased the Englishmen.

The day came. The chief arrived. He brought a gift with him, a deer to roast for a feast. But he also had about a hundred warriors fully armed with bows and arrows. He signaled the whites to put down their arms, and they did so hesitatingly. But they only laid them at their feet, where the weapons could be quickly recovered.

While the tantalizing aroma of venison roasting over the flame wafted to their nostrils, the Englishmen envisioned a feast of good will. But things simply did not fall into place. With displeasure the Algonkians eyed the palisade being built—one that resembled a fort of permanence. They also took exception to the weapons the whites carried, which shot slugs of lead and sounded like thunder. At the same time the Englishmen looked with jaundiced eye at the many arrows in each quiver and bows strung for instant use. Despite an attempt of friendliness by both groups, the air was full of tension.

Indians and whites remained segregated—with the first row of each only a few feet part. In his curiosity, apparently, a warrior picked up a white man's musket to examine it. His intention was misinterpreted by the owner, who quickly grabbed the loaded weapon from the startled guest. To add fuel to the fire, the white man somewhat manhandled the surprised Indian. Another warrior then rushed the Englishman. Guns were quickly snatched and the oncoming feast forgotten.

Control of the groups suddenly got out of hand. Bowstrings, arrows set, were pulled back on one side while muskets were pointed at the Indians on the other side. Threatening gestures followed. Angered, the chief signaled his sullen warriors to depart. Backing into the forest, they watched the whites' every move as they withdrew.

Work at the English settlement during the hot, humid days of summer continued. Minor differences constantly grew to gigantic discords. The palisade seemed airless. Mosquitoes, bearing dreaded malaria, came in swarms, hungry for human blood. Weakened by fever, the men staggered and, after a few swings, dropped the ax. Hunger crept closer as food supplies disappeared. Fish were in the river, but no able-bodied men were available to cast a line. Deer were in the woods but everyone feared to enter with Indians on watch. Arrows continued to sail into the stockade. Every strange sound in the night brought a sleeping man to his feet shouting an alarm. Each crackle and rustle could be the slinking approach of an Indian warrior. The settlers never were sure that the howl of a wolf or the screech of an owl was not an Indian call for an attack, and each day settlers strained their eyes peering into the distance for sight of the sail of a boat bringing supplies from England. As the days wore on, more people died from fever.

But then came autumn! Bright splashes of yellowing aspens pockmarked the woods. Cool winds blew along the broad James River. Fevers subsided. Wild geese and ducks, flight after flight, came, with the birds easily taken. No Indians now were visible in the surrounding forest; thus security was relaxed. But it was a trick, a stunning deception! The Indians, hidden, were on watch. When the leader of the settlement entered the forest, he was captured and dragged to Powhatan's camp for trial. Only the mighty chief of the Algonkians could decide his fate!

As Smith was brought into the Indian camp with clothing in shreds, women and children feared the "pale-skinned ghost"—all except Princess Pocahontas. Viewing him in utter amazement, she felt sorry for the captive. His eyes were "as blue as the sky." She thought he was the bravest person she ever saw. Hurriedly painting her face a shocking red like those of the warriors, she jumped into her ceremonial robe of white turkey feather and took her place beside her father, sitting in judgment on the white prisoner. Who was the man, she wondered. He was none other than Capt. John Smith, the courageous leader of Jamestown, she learned later.

Powhatan, a tall, athletic, stately man, sat erect, unmoving. Around his neck hung a necklace of pearls. His powerful arms were covered with rare copper bracelets. Around him a massive robe of raccoon skins with tails hung. At a glance Captain Smith knew the usefulness of such a garment. In the mottled sunlight within a forest, the black- and buff-colored skin and tails gave Powhatan a near-perfect camouflage.

When the trial began, Powhatan's face was lined and grim. The puissant medicine man with his supposedly supernatural powers and the keeper of sacred arrows had just told Powhatan the white man was "bad medicine." Nonetheless, Smith faced the chief bravely and with words and signs answered questions fearlessly. *Father will let him live*, thought Pocahontas. Little did she know the coming verdict of the counselors, the grizzled warriors of yes-

Indian chief—proud, confident.

teryear, judging the prisoner. When their leader shouted, "The spirits tell us the magic of the paleface man is evil! The prisoner must die!" Pocahontas was worried. But she knew her father, Chief Powhatan, could override the decision of the counselors; still—he made no move. She must act quickly to save the prisoner, but how?

Preparations were made to kill the captain. As he was kneeling, his head placed on a sacrificial stone with arms tied behind his back so that selected warriors could beat him to death, Pocahontas rushed forward, throwing herself atop Smith to protect him. This instantaneous demonstration by Pocahontas stunned and angered the medicine man and counselors. They were not the chief judge, however—Powhatan was. Shouting, Pocahontas pleaded for Smith's life. She agreed to adopt him. And she did!

Powhatan knew the rules of the tribe well. An Indian maiden could save a prisoner from death only through adoption. Fast friends Smith and Pocahontas became, although he was much older. He took time to explain new things to her, and she hungered to learn. His box compass, for instance, with the little spirit inside that made the needle always point to magnetic north fascinated her. She used it continually as they walked in the forest, familiarizing themselves with each other's language and vigilantly observing trees, birds, and mammals.

Powhatan, impressed with Captain Smith's knowledge and that Pocahontas liked him so much, began calling him "my son." He then released his prisoner so he could return to Jamestown, though before Smith left he pulled from his buckskin shirt pocket a string of blue beads that he gave to Pocahontas. Thrilled, she wore the blue beads day and night. Her favorite color she said they were, and they reminded her of the captain's blue eyes.

With Captain Smith now an adopted son, Powhatan began viewing the colonists with greater consideration. *Why take by force that which you can obtain through friendship?* he reasoned. *I am not so simple that I do not know it is better to work with the white people and, being their friend, obtain fine iron hatchets and whatever else we may need.*

So with Captain Smith back in Jametown, Pocahontas's heart was broken and she became a sad princess. Nothing new to learn! She longed to hear more about the strange white people and far-off England.

And the cold of winter came! Food, in short supply at Jamestown by mid-winter, became scarcer as the season wore away. Plagued with inefficiency, the colonists became hungry and weak. Pocahontas begged to divide their food with the whites. But the Indian camp itself had only enough food stored to make it through the winter. This was Indian tradition! Still, Powhatan agreed to provide some food. But only the amount Pocahontas could carry to Jamestown. Crafty Powhatan was sure she could not make the winter trip. But she thought otherwise. Baskets were filled with precious maize and carried all the way to Jamestown. Pocahontas and her girl friends realized the amazing secret of happiness—doing a loving deed for someone. Powhatan's strategy had backfired.

Enough cannot be said about how thankful the settlers were when the maize arrived. Now there was food! Pocahontas's kindly feelings toward Captain Smith, her adopted son, forced her to weather the severe hardships of the trip. She was so happy to see him again, as he always cheered her up.

Later, Pocahontas and her friends made a second trip to Jamestown with food.

But Chief Powhatan was less than pleased with feeding the English at the expense of his own people. "They are like children," he growled, "expecting others to care for them!" While he did not countenance violence at this time, he was even more irritated when Smith, whose unenviable position could be described as that of one having the least leprosy in a leper colony, sailed with his men up the James River in early spring with cannon fully exposed on board. The Englishmen asked for maize—in fact, demanded it. Powhatan did not take kindly to the threatening gesture of the cannon—he sold them little and made them pay an exorbitant price.

Spring the following year, due to a poor autumn harvest, the Indians themselves were short of maize. Many went hungry, and hungry people are cross. Food was rationed. Powhatan allowed himself no more food than others in camp, yet Captain Smith came for more maize, demanded it, and threatened the Indians when his request was refused. Powhatan felt he had delivered on all promises he never made. At this stage the chief turned ominous and shouted, "Powhatan takes orders from no man!" Then suddenly he hid his anger. With a friendly gesture he warmly asked the Englishmen to spend the night. They could discuss the matter the next morning.

He asked the men to stay in the long hut built for guests located at the far end of camp. His strategy? He would have his warriors murder the Englishmen while they slept.

Exhausted from the journey, the whites soon were asleep. But then a suspicious noise outside the hut awakened Smith, who jumped to his feet, rushed to the entrance, and pushed back the bearhide cover. There, in the dim light of darkness he saw a basket and backpack. In the basket was maize, in the backpack a quarter of venison.

Then a soft voice spoke. It was Pocahontas. "Do not stay!" she whispered. "My father means ill—his mood is unfriendly! This is all the food I could carry. Take it and leave immediately for Jamestown!" Then she disappeared into the shadows of the forest. Once again Pocahontas had saved John Smith's life.

Powhatan was fit to be tied! His quarry had slipped away. Embittered, he refused to deal with the men of Jamestown. No longer would he allow Pocahontas to visit the place. And the princess missed Captain Smith more by the day.

Then word came to her that he had been seriously injured in a gunpowder explosion. A warrior spying on the camp said Smith was either dead or dying when carried aboard a ship that set sail for England, and Pocahontas grew sad, but, like a true daughter of her race, bore her grief uncomplainingly.

As more white people came to the land of the Algonkinans, Powhatan visualized serious trouble ahead. Clashes between the two races were more frequent. Their views differed on almost everything. One Indian camp, then another turned cool to those they openly called trespassers. Their friendship now was irreparably damaged. Gradually the Indians began to distrust the whites—finally they hated them. Unknowingly, the whites had themselves in more hot water than a two-hour lobster!

To emphasize his displeasure, Powhatan captured three men of Jamestown and held them prisoner. With Captain Smith no longer in the village, the Englishmen in retaliation kidnapped Pocahontas. They said they would release her only after the chief returned the white prisoners unharmed.

But the men of Jamestown failed to realize the power of Powhatan—one who could not be forced to do anything. He was the law of the forest! Though he loved his little princess dearly, he would release the white prisoners only when supplied with many guns, "the sticks that shoot lightning and thunder as they kill."

For Pocahontas, captivity was easy to bear. She agreed to remain at Jamestown until released; thus no watch was kept. They knew she was impeccably honest. Soon she became a favorite of everyone, especially the women who had come to join the growing settlement. She was taught to weave and spin—a craft so unlike making clothing from deerskin. She was taken to church and learned that the religion of the colonists agreed with her own. There *was* a Great Spirit over all, and one *must* live a good life—helping others and being kind. She learned some of the refinements of white society. She was given a fine dress with wide skirts, stays, puffed sleeves and high lace collar and wore it well. Still, Pocahontas was more comfortable in her white feather-soft deerskin garment and moccasins.

Impressed with the Church of England, Pocahontas decided to become a Christian. Baptized at Jamestown, she was given the English name Rebecca.

Months passed. No word was heard from Captain Smith. He vanished without a trace. Then word came to Pocahontas that he was dead. The gunpowder wound had killed him.

Among Pocahontas's many friends in the rapidly growing Jamestown settlement was a young man, John Rolfe, the son of a family with prestige in England. He fell in love with Pocahontas and asked her to be his wife. He promised to take her to England someday, the land she talked so much about. She agreed to marry him if her father agreed.

The wedding was in Jamestown. Chief Powhatan did not come, for never again would the mighty chieftain set foot in the white man's village. But many of her Indian relatives and friends did attend.

Time passed. Pocahontas had a baby boy who greatly pleased both whites and Indians. He was darker than a white baby and paler than an Indian. To Pocahontas and John he was the most beautiful child in the whole world. Indians came to view him, saying, "Oh, he will become darker as he grows older." Whites said the opposite: "Oh, he will become whiter when he grows up." But to the parents his color was perfect. By now John Rolfe had a fine log house for Pocahontas, and with their child, named Thomas, happiness was complete.

Indian Trail Tree—Broken as a sapling, this maple has marked the direction of the trail for untold generations.

Courtesy of the Wisconsin Department of Natural Resources

John took wife and child to England to visit his family and to see the country so much on his wife's mind. Now she would see the wondrous things Captain Smith had told her about. Powhatan too was pleased, but for a different reason. He wanted a report on the land white men called England. So he sent one of his most trusted braves to accompany his daughter, saying slyly, "four eyes can see more than two."

While in England, Pocahontas learned that Captain Smith was not dead as reported at Jamestown. He came to see her, but she coolly turned her head. She was offended because he had sent no word to her that he was alive. Yet the two became reconciled. It was said that seeing Captain Smith, her adopted son, again pleased Pocahontas more than anything else during her visit, even more than being honored by the queen.

As soon as Powhatan's trusted brave landed in England, he began to cut notches on a stick the chief sent with him. In fact, the chief sent several sticks and ordered the warrior to cut a notch for every Englishman he saw. Then when the brave would return, Powhatan would count the notches and know how many men were in England.

The Indian cut notches and more notches, but the faster he worked, the more men came into view. Soon he ran out of sticks. Hurrying into a nearby woods, he gathered more sticks. Then he again began notching and did more notching. Finally he quit in disgust. Men were everywhere!

Viewing England, Pocahontas at times could hardly believe her eyes. She saw London Bridge, the one Captain Smith told her about. Along the bridge were houses—some as high as the tallest trees in the forest back home. White swans swam on the river. All around were beautiful flowers and trees with strange, sweet fruit.

The ladies of England opened their hearts to Pocahontas. Banquets were given in her honor. English people were enchanted by her beauty and intelligence. They took her to the theater to see plays by William Shakespeare. She enjoyed the parties and the good people, but the chilly, damp climate did not agree with her. Having no resistance to white man's diseases, she turned pale and grew silent. Thinking she was homesick for Jamestown and her people of the forest, her husband engaged passage for them on a ship to America. During her last days in England, Pocahontas was stricken with an unidentified respiratory ailment and her health deteriorated. Homeward bound, the ship docked at Gravesend for fresh water and food supplies. Doctors advised her husband that she was too weak to continue the trip. Put ashore at Gravesend, she died on March 21, 1617, at twenty-two years and was buried the same day in the Chancel of St. George's Church.

Today tourists who come to the Kentish town along the Thames River, twenty miles east of London, can see at the Parish Church of St. George a life-size bronze statue of the Algonkian girl in her tribal dress, a churchyard dedicated as a memorial in her honor, a pair of Pocahontas-theme windows in the east wall of the church, a tombstone with a plaque to Pocahontas, and a four-page folder titled *The Story of Princess Pocahontas*.

Little Thomas Rolfe, her son, attended school in England. Later he returned to Virginia to the very house his father built for Pocahontas. Today several distinguished Americans are descendants of Thomas Rolfe—half Indian, half white—whose mother was an eminent Algonkian Princess.

In her honor a fine oil painting titled *Pocahontas* hangs in the national Capitol building in Washington. It shows her being baptized into Christianity. Actually, she lived a Christian life long before her baptism.

When fame no longer could be denied Pocahontas, a few mythmaker writers went to work piling legends on her until the girl herself can hardly be recognized. But Pocahontas will always be remembered for having befriended the people of Jamestown—the first permanent English settlement in North America. It was the little princess who saved the settlers from starvation and from extermination by Indians who turned enemy as soon as they realized their domain was in jeopardy.

The death of Pocahontas deeply shocked the Algonkians as well as the people of Jamestown. Heavy with sorrow, chief Powhatan died within a year. Without their powerful leader the tribe had neither unity of purpose nor organized manpower to save themselves and slowly disintegrated. Not even their fellowmen of the forest came to assist them, for Indian solidarity at the time was as nonexistent as white man's understanding.

Colonists took to work with a vengeance. Armed with all the power science of that day could supply, the whites moved forward, gradually pushing the people of the forest into oblivion and acquiring their homeland. It was a dark day for the Algonkians.

IV

Nothing but Prairie and Sky

Born during turbulent 1776, the United States was a nation east of the Mississippi River fashioned by white men. The land of destiny beyond, called the Great West, was a beckoning, mysterious prairie land tailored by nature itself, whose full dimension no man had measured, whose interior no white man yet had seen. Territory invaded by courageous traders, few at most, hazily reported on what they saw.

The Great West! Nothing but prairie and sky, or so it seemed they said—an endless land that dwarfed a man until he thought only of eternity. It stretched without end to distant mountains snow-capped forever, whose peaks seem to hold up the sky. It grew grass eyeball high to a man and bison in numbers beyond belief. And there were Indians "as tough as a chunk of dried jerky" the beaver trappers said—sometimes friendly, sometimes murderous, but always suspicious and suspect.

But this vast prairieland of mystery and myth from Mexico to Canada and from the Mississippi River to the Rocky Mountains was claimed by a nation across the sea—France. The power on the throne, Napoleon I, living on a diet of war, needed ready cash, not land. And he got it! For a mere $15 million the Great West became the property of the United States when Napoleon agreed to the Louisiana Purchase. President Jefferson received the good news by air mail in 1803—a carrier pigeon flew the message from New York to Washington.

Almost before the ink dried on the paper, Jefferson covertly arranged to explore this Great West, seeking an overland route to the Pacific Ocean and on to the rich China trade. His objective was as fixed as the points of a compass. Though utter fantasy, if successful the dream would change fiction to fact.

LEWIS AND CLARK ROUTE, 1804–1806.

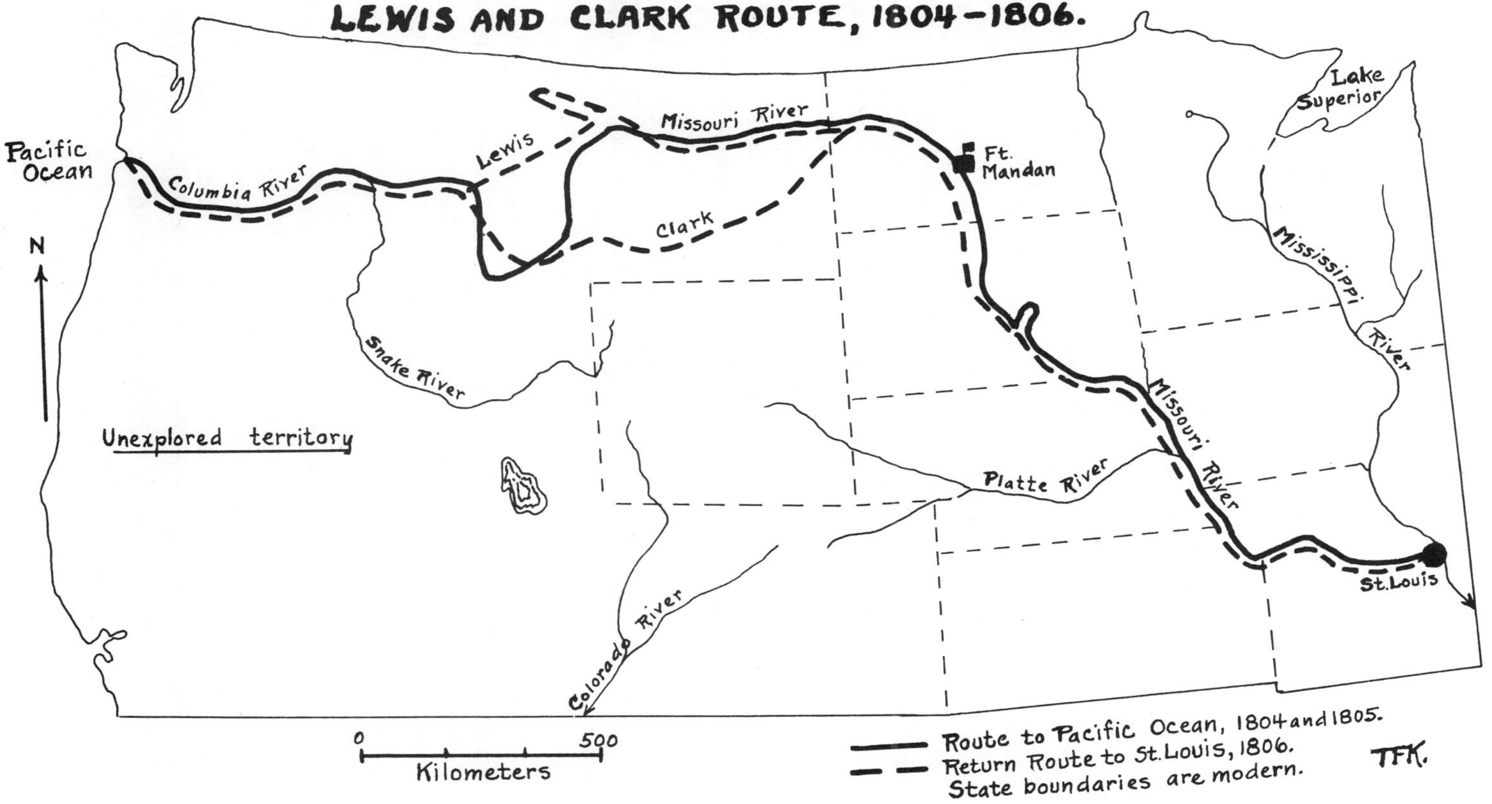

So on to the Rocky Mountains! Here were peaks, as one approaches them around a bend of a winding Indian path, that literally explode into view. More rugged and majestic than any mountains east of the Mississippi River, they soar and climb to the sky—forming an ever-changing spectrum. One blinks, vainly trying to bring it all into focus. Gray and white, then purple, then softly blurred by rain and snow, their changing hues can best be perceived when tuned to one's imagination.

Our early presidents were men of foresight and wisdom. Take President Jefferson! In no time after the Louisiana Purchase, Jefferson had a well-conceived plan. He would fashion an expedition to go west and its leader would be none other than Capt. Meriwether Lewis, a young man of rare ability—quiet, qualified, trustworthy.

Thomas Jefferson had sufficient opportunity to evaluate the bravery, intellect, tact, and imagination of Meriwether Lewis long before he selected him as leader of the expedition. Jefferson and Lewis were neighbors in Albemarle County, Virginia. From earliest childhood Lewis studied the natural wonders of his country—exploring, hunting, fishing—and after his father's death he managed his mother's farms. During the Whiskey Insurrection he served the nation as an officer. One of his fellow officers was William Clark, younger brother of the renowned general George Rogers Clark, a Revolutionary War hero. The two young men became close and trusted friends. Lewis chose William Clark, perhaps the most competent man in the nation, as partner. Lewis promised Clark an equal voice in all decisions, and so the Lewis and Clark Expedition was formed.

Congress, everything but generous with money in those days, appropriated the paltry sum of $2,500.00 to the expedition—about enough for Band-Aids today. Army posts, however, contributed a few supplies. Heaviest cargo would be lead for bullets and the short rifles made special. Included was a surprise weapon—the newly invented swivel cannon. Instruments of many kinds would be taken and flint, powder, and medicine. Presents for Indians were many—beads, pendants, mirrors, medals, iron axes, and knives. But no stockpile of blue beads, a favorite of western Indians, Lewis and Clark learned later, was included. Could it be the blue sky of the Great West made Plains Indians prefer blue over any other color?

From Saint Louis, a village of few frontier families, on a rare and glorious morning, the expedition started grinding up the unpredictable Missouri River. A solitary eagle came off a tree branch as if summoned, majestically sailing through the river mist on powerful whispering wings. Soft clouds sat on an air blanket. The earth smelled freshly fragrant. A hint of spring filled the air. It was May 14, 1804. Besides the two captains there were fourteen soldiers of the regular army, nine Kentucky volunteers, a famed hunter, two indispensable French rivermen, and York, Clark's black servant. These were all handpicked men who shot straight, thought, and talked with a straight tongue. They prided themselves as fighters of excellence—that enemies might kill them, but would never make them give up. And this boast they made good!

An iron-framed keelboat fifty-five feet long, carrying twenty-two oars and a small sail, was the principal ship of three. Boats were rowed, poled, pushed, or sailed against the ever-changing Missouri River current. Guards posted nights prevented surprise attacks by hostiles. It seems somehow, intuitively, the captains foresaw trouble before it arose. But trouble would come and in many forms!

Seldom were all members of the expedition on the boat. Clark, the better riverman, personally directed the keelboat during the early stages. Lewis, following winding Indian trails along shore, collected flora and took notes. Drewyer, interpreter, trapper, and hunter accompanied Lewis. Hurrying to remain within sight of the boats, the two fought willow thickets, stumbled over hummocks, and waddled through wetlands. At day's end, clothes wet and torn, they resembled refugees from a chain gang.

Ah! this indomitable Missouri—carrying the Indian name "Large Canoes," as only crafts this size can master its water. The Missouri—colossal and treacherous, broad and turbid, with eddies, sandbars, and islands that grow and suddenly vanish. This tempestuous Missouri—constantly restless, channels changing, banks building on one shore, disappearing on the other. Forests were established, bewilderingly undermined, and swept away. Yes, this obstinate Missouri, water charged with mud and sand, forcefully moved into the unknown. Logs broken, ends set in mud like a military abatis, were aimed to ram any object brazen enough to challenge its churning water.

Operating the boats required skill of superior degree. Quick decisions became a way of life, despite the fact that any wrong judgment could wreck the expedition. Lack of an interpreter who could converse with all Indian tribes, each with its own dialect, also was a handicap. But no man alive had such qualifications.

The first major crisis struck in today's South Dakota when an overwhelming force of belligerent Sioux warriors armed to the teeth forced the expedition to stop to pay ransom. For three days Clark, the arbitrator, had not a wink of sleep. But trouble had been anticipated. White traders, surrounded by the powerful Sioux at this point, were forced to dispose of their goods at ruinous low prices—set by the Sioux themselves. The traders painfully interpreted the deal as nothing less than uncompromising robbery. Seeing that the Indians could not be dissuaded from their exorbitant demands, Lewis and Clark brought the repeating swivel cannon into play. Electrified by the sudden show of force, the Sioux disappeared faster than a Janaury heat wave. Here was a prime example of the overwhelming respect force achieves. The Teton Sioux got the message! They learned that a new breed of white rivermen were using the Missouri—men who would not be bluffed or bullied.

Mandan Interior, by George Catlin
Courtesy of the New York Historical Society, New York City.

Buffalo Chase (Sioux), by George Catlin.

News of white man's power flashed through the Sioux underground more rapidly than the boats advanced up river. This awesome show of force by the determined explorers may explain why the Sioux never again molested them during the several hundred miles through their territory. After this unprecedented experience with the cannon, Sioux warriors avoided the expedition like a prairie rattler colony.

On October 27, 1804, a village of Mandan Indians, a tribe practicing primitive agriculture, was reached. Friendly to white traders, who hadn't ventured beyond this point, and their Sioux neighbors, the tribe lived in two permanent villages of large dome-shaped earthen lodges supported by timbers. Earlier, the tribe inhabited nine populous villages downstream near present-day Mandan, North Dakota. There they suffered from disease, especially smallpox, brought by white traders. Possessing no resistance, the disease struck them down. Taking advantage of their weakened condition, Sioux forced the tribe to move upstream to a less desirable location.

Winter was endured at Fort Mandan, an improvised government stronghold near the Mandan village. The inevitable victory of spring over a bitter winter was celebrated. River ice disappearing, the expedition continued its upstream journey. Three new members were added: Sacajawea, a beautiful sixteen-year-old Indian maiden; her baby; and Toussaint Charbonneau, her French husband hired as interpreter. Sacajawea, who belonged to a western band of Shoshones living on the east slope of the Rocky Mountains, was the key. Captured by a Hidatsa Indian raiding party, she had been brought to their village several hundred miles down the Missouri. Later she was sold to Charbonneau.

Bucking the unconquerable current of a swollen Missouri, the party advanced into the land of the setting sun—land so level twilight extends into night. Horizons are vague; earth and sky merge, with colors fading to pale pastels. Here was country completely foreign to white men. Somewhere ahead were mountains, but where? And how could they overcome this insurmountable barrier with no packhorses to transport equipment and food? Sacajawea thought she had the answer. She knew her people had horses and agreed to talk to them. But could the expedition find her tribe? Not much chance! The land was endless.

Traveling with Sacajawea in the party was a pleasure. She endured hardship without a murmur. She was intelligent and she was cheerful. Effervescing optimism, Sacajawea encouraged a countdown to success. As days wore on, Lewis and Clark were struck by her phenomenal memory. Though only eleven years old when taken prisoner, she remembered landmarks en route precisely. She carried her two-month-old baby, Jean-Baptiste, the baby who never cried, strapped to a cradle-board. Crew favorites they were in every respect but name. Finding their names difficult to pronounce, the crewmen called them Janey and Pompey.

Brilliant, moody, introspective, Captain Lewis at thirty years was a hardy frontiersman mainly of Welsh descent. Knowledgeable of flora east of the Mississippi, he was self-taught for the most part, even in medicine. He would treat the many sick and wounded almost like a physician.

Cut from another cloth, Captain Clark, of Scotch descent, was outgoing and good-natured, a redhead who drove himself to the point of exhaustion. His disposition was pleasant and controlled.

Thirty-four years old, a capable mapper, surveyor, and geographer, he expressed himself clearly in writing, though, like Lewis, his spelling was not a strong point. The courage of the two captains was astounding, their character strong as granite. They always had lived with danger so took it for granted.

York, the black man of the party, was a jovial soul, materially poor though spiritually rich. Indians who never before had seen a white man, then suddenly saw several in one group were completely puzzled to see a black man. Not too strangely, they thought the Great Spirit had undercooked the white ones and burned the one who was black. Those with brown skin themselves, of course, were done just right. To keep the curious Indians guessing, York told them he put the black paint on his skin himself and asked a warrior to try to rub it off. While the Indian rubbed and rubbed, York was in heaven. He told him the paint would outlast anything the Indians could make. After much rubbing, the Indian agreed.

Engaging sounds of nature filled the air. Bugling of sandhill cranes, winging their way northward, swept the flat landscape, and cranes, as paraphrased from Aldo Leopold, are beautiful "beyond the reach of words." Their weird, engaging sound carried for miles. Listening closely, one could detect its unison nature: the male producing one note and the female another in a way that they sounded like a solo instead of a duet.

And what was going on in Sacajawea's mind en route? Not a prisoner on this trip, she was delighted to go westward toward her childhood home. Like other Indians, she had loved her childhood despite days of physical discomfort and hunger. Then, too, she was accepted by these white people as a human being and not a savage. Even her husband now held her in higher esteem. Her charming baby, whom everyone loved, especially Clark, made her extremely happy.

Tragedy repeatedly hounded the expedition. One midnight the guard hoarsely shouted the men awake; the sandbar on which they were encamped was disintegrating rapidly. The treacherous Missouri, again on a collision course, was going wild. Looking back while fleeing to the boats, Lewis and Clark saw their campsite quickly disappear under the turbid water. Another lesson: Never trust the Big Muddy!

For the crew, manning the boats day in and day out was grueling, killing work. Here was a crew described as a gang of misfits by many back home who saw it assemble. But tough they were. Lewis himself insisted that the men were totally dedicated, and praise coming from him, one not given to overstatements, was like praise coming from Caesar. Fifteen dismal miles were averaged per day—no more. Those who walked the shore taking notes hunted wildlife also, as fresh meat was necessary to satisfy the crew's overpowering appetite. With a menu changing continually, now it included delicacies such as beaver tails and livers and wild goose eggs. And Sacajawea was a prime contributor, continually bringing foods never before eaten by the crew—artichokes, for instance. Knowing that field mice collect and store them in caches, she found the caches and dug the artichokes from the soil with a pointed stick.

But now the expedition was moving into grizzly bear country, and grizzly bears—self-proclaimed guardians of the real estate they occupy—abhor pressure from any source. These beasts of the wild especially hated humans; thus those of the expedition who walked the riverbank were vulnerable to attack. Forced to run for their very lives, they learned a lesson or two when dealing with these giant killers. They learned that a grizzly's size and awkward gait was no handicap. It could run like a horse, but unlike a horse could do so over exceedingly rough terrain and through heavy brush. Those walking the shore discovered that a person had little time to seek refuge. And where? Up trees! Although black bears can climb trees, grizzlies cannot. This lesson saved several lives.

Another lesson acquired by persons walking the shore was their own personal speed. They had never known they could run to a nearby tree and make it up the trunk to the top so fast. Though safe from attack, a person found himself entrapped while the boats proceeded up the river. And stranded a person was! The big brutes usually sat or lay next to the tree trunk waiting for hours, knowing that that two-legged intruder sitting among the branches must come down sometime. And a musket in the hand of a man walking the riverbank was of little value. Lead balls fired into a grizzly wouldn't stop him; thus, to play it safe, musket was dropped and it was full speed ahead to the nearest tree.

And then the bison—those shaggy bovines walking through an ocean of prairie grass—dotted the terrain, but bothered no one unless angered. Just as a grizzly bear is mean enough to sleep where he wants, so is a bison herd tough enough to go where it chooses. Bison gave the boats no more than a passing glance. Crewmen could see domineering bulls, fighting for top status in the herd, strike heads, groan, bellow, and push until the weaker one retreated. Yet the winner never pursued the loser in an attempt to injure him. Bulls along the riverbank not fighting amused themselves by driving their powerful horns into the high bank and throwing soil on their backs in an attempt to drive away bothersome insects.

This bovine of the Great West was a combination of strength and timidity, magnificent in its distorted proportion. As tall as an Indian at its shaggy hump, a bull stood ten feet long and weighed a ton. With powerful teeth and jaws, he cropped grass so short a season was needed for it to recover. On land never-ending, married to nothing but grass below and sky above, vast, earth-shaking herds multiplied with surprising rapidity. To the Plains Indians, the bison was everything. This was proven three generations later; with the bison wiped from the plains by white man, the downfall of Indian tribes of the American West was complete.

The Iron Horse encounters buffalo.

Canada geese choose the easy flying formation.

    Then winged creatures, introducing spring, provided the expedition with beauty and food. Something told the geese to fly north to their nesting grounds, so, floating gracefully through the air, flocks of Canada geese arrowed their way along the age-old Missouri river flyway. Most birds migrate in silence—not geese. Old ganders, cautious and wise, offer repetitious encouragement to the females[1] as the flock advances in the arrowpoint formation used by large birds with appreciable natural intelligence. Each bird helps the one following by intentionally leaving a strong updraft behind its wingtips. Beginning with the leader, which has none of this assistance, the bird following on either side places itself to take

---

[1]Geese and many other large-bird species mate for life.

advantage of this lift. By doing so it flies with the least possible effort. Should a bird fly ahead of this position, it would immediately sense the increased workload and quickly drop back into the proper slot, and if it lagged behind, doing less work than its rightful share, the bird following would let out an immediate response. And Lewis and Clark were men who understood the honk of geese as a magic sound, a sound coming from self-propelled air travelers who view humans as undesirables. Still the honking echo of geese signals another season, and long after the gabble ends their sound haunts one's heart.

The boats moved on, and among nature's wonders crewmen viewed the greatness of vastness. Riveted to their thankless task, the gang hung tough. "Away, you rolling river!" Work was never-ending. Without warning, windstorms struck the Missouri, reaching violent gales in minutes. Hitting the flotilla one late afternoon, angry winds tore the sail from the captain's keelboat. Hard by the shore, a gnarled oak, with crown twisting and creaking, took no notice of the gale that challenged the magnificent silence. Ma Nature, surly and rebellious, whipped uncontrollable waves into a churning frenzy, washing Lewis's and Clark's irreplaceable notes overboard. While the captains fought the waters to keep the ship afloat, Sacajawea, with little Pompey in the cradle-board basket on her back, was busy as a bee collecting nectar from a prairie rose. Hanging to the side of the restless boat with one hand, with the other she was calmly retrieving from the churning water all the priceless papers she could reach. This act of kindness touched the hearts of the captains, who had worked endlessly recording previously unknown environmental features and new botanical finds as the expedition moved from white civilization. Tense moments these were! Finally the wind subsided and the sun eluded capture by the clouds, presenting a scene perhaps as heartwarming as it was to Noah catching a glimpse of sunlight after forty days of rain. All boats remained afloat, but damage was heavy. Repairs made, the expedition again moved forward.

Hardship became a way of life. Come night, with the expedition members utterly exhausted, camp was made. Crewmen oftentimes were unable to give a hand. Not a day passed that everyone was free of illness or injury. Sinewy, hardy, and self-reliant, crewmen forced themselves to be both daring and adventurous, and the passing of years imprinted deep lines on their faces that symbolized dangers confronted and hardships uncomplainingly endured. Sprains, bruises, fever, injured backs, strained muscles, and abdominal pains were continuous. During daylight the party was plagued by no-seeums, flies, gnats, wasps, and yellow jackets. On land, snakes held their ground—coiling, striking. And grizzlies, ready to slash one to ribbons, appeared at inopportune moments.

With his usual foresight, Captain Lewis had placed in the keelboat at Saint Louis a wooden chest containing medicine. Having studied medicine at home, he remembered a number of local remedies. Along the way he treated at one time or other every person in the party, including himself. When Sacajawea took sick after two months of travel, everyone worried, as she hovered between life and death for days. The expedition moved on, the captains tending her in relays. While one walked the shore taking notes, the other treated her on boat. And the crew during this period was a depressed band of journeymen. Sacajawea's optimism and her cheerful helpfulness were sorely missed. When she recovered, the crew spirit zoomed skyward and the men returned to normal efficiency.

But then Lewis unexpectedly took ill. The treatment he prescribed called for a brew made from boiled chokecherry leaves and bark. After drinking a quart of the bitter concoction, which one might think could kill a field of giant ragweed, he improved. Gradually the fever abated and abdominal pain subsided. This remedy his mother had taught him in their native Virginia.

Continuing up the snakelike Missouri, the expedition reached the land of the capricious Blackfeet, who for generations fought the Sioux for the lush northern grassland black with bison. The stream was now narrowing and dividing—travel with the three boats soon would end. And it did!

A demanding search for large cottonwood trees was first and foremost. Found and felled, they were hollowed into thirty-foot-long dugouts. To save the boats for the return journey (highly uncertain at this point), they were sunk in a deep pool. In the much smaller dugouts more memories than personal possessions were taken with them.

As they traveled on and on, miles and miles to nowhere were covered. Rapids and falls were encountered, seemingly at the most troublesome places. Portaging—the cumbersome dugouts were

Striking Back, by John Mason Brown.

dragged, pushed, and carried. Bruised and exhausted, the party struggled ten days to cover a painful eighteen miles. Adding to and compounding their miseries, no one had sleep while encamped on a small island. Silver-tipped grizzlies, reaching for their most impolite manners, harassed them from dusk to dawn.

As they journeyed through the land of the powerful, obstreperous Blackfeet, strangely, there were no Indians. Indian sign, yes—Indians, no! Was it a trick—keeping hidden, hoping the whites would drop their guard? Old hands were aware of such stratagems. The air was full of tension. Conditions dictated a surprise night attack, so night guards were doubled. Still no Indians! The Blackfeet, like the Sioux, apparently had no desire to mix with these roughnecks and their cannon.

Clark's alert eye on July 19 spotted an abandoned Indian camp. Sacajawea, walking with him at the time, noticed trees stripped of their bark and knew the sign—Indians had removed the coarse outer bark to reach the edible inner portion. Unexpectedly, a deafening roar in an unseen gorge ahead struck them. A waterfall—and what a picture, mountain-pure water cascading down a vast abyss. It was as beautiful as a heavenly dream, and anyone who viewed it ran the risk of having his spirit stolen by the mystical charmer. For a moment the party reveled in this gorgeous scene and its breathtaking beauty, unmindful of the torturous struggle ahead, pulling, carrying, pushing, dragging boats and supplies over and around the exquisite gorge near today's Helena, Montana. Conquered with agonizing effort, this waterfall and canyon made so great an impression on the captains they named it Gates of the Mountains. Its shocking magnificence froze to their memory! The next day they saw a valley of astounding beauty in the distance—trees blushing red, others old gold. From it rose a cloud of smoke. Was the smoke from an Indian camp, or was it a phenomenon of nature? More travel brought Indian signs that helped to fan the flame of hope. Where a small stream ran into the Missouri, Sacajawea stopped suddenly, recognizing where her tribe collected white soil for paint. "We will reach the fork in a few moons," she assured Lewis and Clark. Those walking now encountered a tough woody shrub with thorns, the prickly pear, that tore clothing and flesh alike.

As Sacajawea predicted, Three Forks of the Missouri—far beyond any point previously reached by white men—confronted them. Lewis and Clark now had tested foothills of the commanding mountain range the expedition must conquer to reach the Pacific Ocean. No question! "To move supplies over this rugged Bitterroot Range, horses are as necessary as the air we breathe." Portaging rapids and falls and lugging backpacks, the endless journey slowly was killing the crew. As they climbed sheer precipices, loose rock tumbled down, sending small avalanches of stone cascading into the pathway of those following.

Then a banner day came—July 28. Morale shot to the stratosphere, injecting the party with optimism, when Sacajawea reaffirmed they were on Shoshoni lands. In fact, they were approaching the spot where huts of her people had stood five years earlier when Hidatsa warriors attacked them. Moving on a short distance, she stopped, pointing to a place in midstream where in darkness she had been overtaken while attempting to escape. And she displayed a quiet sadness while reliving her capture and being taken some seven hundred miles down the Missouri to the Hidatsa village. Still Sacajawea showed little emotion—standing alone, inwardly suffering. But she was moved more than anyone knew, and it would surface later during reunion with her people.

As they proceeded up the narrowing, angry river, again it forked. But Sacajawea recognized this portion of the river like her own sweet voice and pointed to the tributary leading to her people. On August 8 she perceived a small plain in the forest—the summer home of her tribe—and assured the captains they would soon arrive at the Shoshoni winter camp.

It should be emphasized here that her northern Shoshones were everything but warlike. Only a few had guns, but the warriors were fine shots with bow and arrow. A small tribe, it remained secluded in the mountain wilderness—avoiding the larger, more powerful tribes of the plains. But the Shoshoni were comparatively rich in some possessions—horses, for instance! And Lewis and Clark longed for those horses. In fact, these beasts of burden stood squarely between expedition success or failure.

Days passed! Boulders, rapids, and waterfalls from a few to several feet high time and again interfered with any forward movement. Continually dragging dugouts around these barriers made further advancement by water in this rugged terrain impractical. Morale dipped to a new low. But then suddenly Sacajawea began jumping up and down with joy, pointing to a column of Indians approaching on horseback. "This is my tribe!" she shouted. They were at a spot near today's Armstead, Montana. After the Indians had escorted the explorers to camp, a meeting between the Shoshoni chief and Lewis and Clark was arranged.

The captains urged, even begged, Sacajawea to come to the chief's hut to act as interpreter. Knowing that Indian women had few rights, she agreed reluctantly. Entering, shyly sitting down, she began to interpret the conversation. Then suddenly she jumped to her feet, ran toward the chief, and embraced him, weeping. She recognized him as her brother Cameahawait. Moved, but to a lesser degree, he held her for a moment—then, in true Indian tradition, emotion was brushed aside, the conference resumed, and Sacajawea returned to her seat. As she again attempted to interpret, tears and sobs interrupted.

After the meeting, Chief Cameahawait told his sister the sad news about their family. It was completely wiped out in the Hidatsa attack except one other brother, away hunting during Sacajawea's short stay, and himself. As boys, they had been taught to run into the woods when an enemy approached, and this had saved their lives. Presents the explorers carried were distributed—beads, metal knives, iron axes, and Jefferson medal pendants. But the cannon was still with them so Clark asked the chief if he wished to hear it fired. He did. The thundering blast stunned the women and children, who ran for cover. Warriors, expecting the worst from the strangers, grabbed their bows and set arrows. As soon as they recovered their composure, York stepped forward and in his low, melodious voice asked a warrior who had been studying him whether he would care to try to rub the black color from his skin. Not understanding English, when Sacajawea translated the message, the warrior got busy working on York's forearm. He rubbed and rubbed without success. Another warrior got busy on York's other arm. Not only did York's black skin draw attention, but his curly hair puzzled all the Shoshones, whose hair, like that of all Indians, was as straight as one of their arrows.

Trading for horses began in earnest on August 18. Of all the articles the Indians wanted, guns, powder, and lead balls, there was no surplus. It soon was apparent that the horse was a warrior's prized possession and none felt he wanted to yield something so dear to him. Cameahawait finally agreed to release a few, but bartering was difficult. Yet without Sacajawea, not a single horse would have been acquired. Her presence and her decision to continue with the expedition thawed the trading chill. At times the bargaining session took on the appearance of a Bowery brawl. Each time, Sacajawea restored cordial relations between the two groups. Though the Shoshones had seven hundred horses, most individually owned by the warriors, bargaining was tough. Promise of future trade, about all Lewis and Clark could offer, moved no warrior who lived from day to day. Still, through Sacajawea's efforts, twenty-nine horses were obtained—only a few in good flesh, however.

Foreseeing the need for dugouts again if their agonizing voyage to the Pacific Ocean proved successful, the crude conveyances were filled with rocks and sunk in a river pool. Loading their meager supplies on the twenty-nine horses, the party began its upward climb along Indian trails and game runs through the rocky, challenging Bitterroot Range.

Before climbing a rugged 1,020 feet, everyone in the party was convinced that without Shoshoni horses the expedition would have failed at this spot. And isolated mountain tribes along the way—hostile to any intruders—permitted the expedition to pass only when they saw an Indian woman struggling along with a baby on her back.

The unbearable climb up the mountainside, which seemingly extended forever, cannot be fully expressed by words. "We ate our very last morsel of provisions except a little portable soup," wrote a crewman, "then killed a wolf and ate it." The land was a horrible mountain desert, as wildlife had moved to the lowland to avoid being submerged in snow. Moody and changeable was the weather. Heavy morning fogs formed deceptive and virtually impenetrable walls. Burning off by midday, cumulus clouds would drift against an azure sky—then without warning the sky would turn sullen and gray, dark and uncompromising. Even the brightest day would turn on a man, conjuring up clouds that fired stinging sleet as though shot from a carbine.

Awesome and remote, the peaks responded with primeval energy of untamed wilderness. Many times the party thought it had reached the mountain divide only to find itself on a lower ridge with the mountaintop in the distance towering above. One horse, then another, loaded with precious supplies, rolled down the mountain never to be seen again. It escaped no one that the climb was slowly killing some of the strongest among them. Despite a series of crises and false starts, the party continued the climb up snowbound trails, knowing the crest was somewhere ahead. Buried in ice and snow, the earth lay dead.

Finally the main divide of the Bitterroot Mountains—today's boundary between Montana and Idaho—was reached. Then there was the view down the valley toward the afternoon sun. Truly a land of paradise! Warm westerly winds transformed the white blanket into tiny ripples of water that sparkled like diamond clusters illuminated in a jeweler's showcase. Quietly tumbling over shiny boulders, the water hastened to keep a date with the ocean. Several party members prayed aloud to God, thanking him for the safe passage to the mountaintop. Miraculously, the secret door through the mountains had been pried open to white man!

Then they followed the precipitous 158-mile Lolo Trail used by Nez Perce Indians, who lived on the western side of the Bitterroot Mountains, to reach the Great Plains for their semiannual bison hunts. This trail, it was learned later, connected the Lewis and Clark Expedition with the Columbia River drainage—and passage to the Pacific.

As they were descending along the turbulent Lochsa Fork of the Clearwater River, Lewis's diary pictures their struggle: "Walking is exceedingly difficult . . . we have been obliged to kill a second colt for food. Our guns are scarcely of service for there is no living creature in the mountains except a few small pheasants [1] and a small species of gray squirrel . . . the men are growing weak and losing flesh fast."

Flashing ahead for a moment to year 1924, three student foresters, Ralph Space, Charles Fox, and myself, threaded our way from Kooskia, Idaho, to the mountain divide along this same Lochsa Fork of the Clearwater River, mapping previously unmapped forest cover and other natural features on that portion of the Selway National Forest[2] for the United States Forest Service long before aerial photography days. With no roads through this wilderness, game trails mostly and the age-old Lolo Trail[3] of Lewis and Clark days were followed. Our packer with his packtrain of a burly saddle horse and six tough mules found travel difficult to a painful degree, as did we who traveled afoot.

But back to 1805 and the Lewis and Clark expedition! Stumbling down the mountainside, the party eventually reaches the Clearwater River. Aches, pains, miseries—yet each step now shrieks confidence. In the distance—a clearing. Were the trees removed by man or nature? Days later the question is answered when they discover an Indian camp under a kind old chief, Twisted Hair. Noticing the crew resembles walking skeletons, Twisted Hair brings them tasty and nourishing dried salmon. The chief answers their prayers as they learn about the uncharted winding route down the Clearwater River to the Snake, thence to the Columbia. "The Colum-

---

[1] Grouse, presumably.
[2] Now the Bitterroot and the Clearwater National Forests.
[3] Called "Buffalo Trail" by Nez Perce Indians, a route they used for generations to cross the mountains to the multitudinous bison herds in today's Montana and Wyoming. Strictly speaking, the Lolo Trail is the travel route from Lolo, Montana, to Weippe, Idaho.

bia," he says with sign language, "flows into the great water." The captains interpret "the great water" as the Pacific Ocean. After sketching the route on a bleached mountain sheep skin, using a colorful plant dye, he carefully rolls it up so it can be easily carried. "But you get to the great water only by boat," he adds. "I keep your horses to when you return."

It was now early October. Autumn fire blazed brilliance as majestic reds and golds of hardwoods spotlighted the greens of conifers. Trees were hurriedly cut and sectioned into logs. Dugouts for the long journey downsteam to "the great water" were hewn. After bucking the Missouri River current from their starting point at the Mississippi River to the Rockies, the party envisioned an easy journey downstream—no current to fight, no portages, no eddies to run, and no towlines to use. Such a thought was just a picturesque dream. Ahead, there were surprises—yes, many surprises!

Rapids were everywhere. With one conquered, another appeared. Dugouts continually struck boulders, then hung there. Hours were lost in disengaging them. Cargo repeatedly spilled into the churning river and defied recovery. Water took much of it ahead, never to be seen again. Clothing and blankets were lost; gunpowder became wet and useless. Precious time was wasted retrieving diminishing supplies. But finally the confluence of the Snake and Columbia rivers was reached.

Far down the Columbia they met six Indians in an uncommonly long canoe, dressed not in buckskin, but, of all things, in white caps and jackets of American sailors. Sailors? Surely not sailors! But there they were, wearing clothing of American sailors. And how did American sailors reach the west coast? Only one way—by sailing entirely around the horn of South America, a precarious trip taking years.

The Pacific surely could not be far away. Confidence zoomed. But delays of one sort or other plagued Lewis and Clark's progress. Weather in the lower Columbia was an enigma—abruptly changing from snow flurries to rain and fog with visibility near zero. And the river current slowed to the point where they were not sure whether the dugouts were moving downstream or up or even moving at all. As they were surrounded by fog, nothing was certain. On and on they went, hoping for the best. Suddenly there it was—the stupendous Pacific, extending endlessly into the heavy haze, rolling, roaring, driving wave after wave against the water of the Columbia River. the expedition surely now had reached "the great water."

Surviving on half-rations for days, mostly dried salmon given them by Chief Twisted Hair and roots of native plants, the party staggered ashore. It was December 1805. Gaunt and weak, three of the strongest men, faithful as salmon after years returning to the stream in which they were born, dragged themselves into the forest in search of food. After being gone two days, they hobbled back, pulling a quarter of elk they had shot. That night there was feasting and singing filled the air. Captain Clark with his red hair aflame by the glow of fire led the merrymaking. Even Captain Lewis, whom none in the party had seen laugh and dance, joined in the excitement. But why not celebrate!? Were they not the first United States expedition to cross the Great West and the Rocky Mountains to the Pacific Ocean? Hadn't they conquered the unknown territory, "beyond the beyond"?

Winter lashed out with fury, hitting them with both barrels. Wind blew madly—in the air, on the ground, on all sides. Even the great Pacific reflected the change with higher and more powerful waves. From the pounding of the surf, profound respect for nature reigned! Encamped on a cliff overlooking the ocean, feasting on fish and meat, bodies again grew strong.

At last—spring! Homeward bound! Dugouts were rowed up the Columbia River, then the Snake and the Clearwater. Fragrances of pine and fir trees, unnoticed on their harrowing westward journey, offered silent messages of encouragement. Evenings the captains finalized their sketches and notes of the country—the first ever—and listed plants, animals, and birds seen. But Indians along the way were anything but friendly, and it was Sacajawea, as usual, who prevented savage warfare between the two groups. At one location a war party halted the expedition, but the chief and warriors were so impressed by the youthful squaw pleading for peace, that bows and lances were lowered and the explorers were permitted to pass.

Chief Twisted Hair's camp was reached. He had kept his word. The horses were well fed and in good flesh. Travel over the mountain divide again would be attempted by horses—dugouts would be left behind. The dreaded Bitterroot Range now was less awesome, and the spring weather proved eminently cooperative compared to the snow and cold during their westward trek. Pushing on toward the Shoshoni camp, Captain Lewis reflected that guns were used in only one instance. Just one man was lost en route, and he died not from an arrow, but from food poisoning.

Arriving at the Shoshoni camp, Sacajawea was given the supreme surprise of her young life. Through Lewis and Clark she was honored for her superior contribution, making the trip to the Pacific successful even beyond their expectations. Shoshoni warriors watching the brief ceremony were stunned, as was Sacajawea. To them, only warriors were given honors, not squaws! But the warriors detected she accepted the honor reluctantly, thus her status in the tribe remained firm.

Soon the expedition was on its way. Loyal to her French husband, Sacajawea accompanied him to their starting point, Mandan Indian village and Fort Mandan. A few Shoshoni traveled with the party to the submerged boats, and horses were returned to Chief Cameahawait as a gift from the United States. When the boats were raised from the river pool, the Shoshones were bade goodbye. Now the expedition divided into two groups; One, under Lewis, went down the Missouri, the other, under Clark who took a new route— the uncharted Yellowstone River. Sacajawea, her husband, and their child went with Captain Clark.

Down the Yellowstone some sixty miles, a giant flat-top rock towered some two hundred feet above the countryside. On a hot summer day Clark climbed to the top. Among pictures of animals and forms painted and carved by Indians over the centuries, with hunting knife he engraved: William Clark, July 25, 1806.

Fort Mandan was reached by both groups about the middle of August. There Charbonneau was paid five hundred dollars. And Sacajawea? Not one cent! But then, being an Indian woman, she expected nothing. She assumed she was appropriately rewarded by serving the expedition and seeing her beloved people, inasmuch as she felt the greatness of her childhood home in her heart. But she had served more than she knew. Lewis and Clark's journals bear testimony to the value of her service.

Before leaving, Captain Clark promised Sacajawea he would pay for Jean-Baptiste's education. And he did! Working out of Fort Bridger, Baptiste in later years became a respected hunter and guide on the Great Plains. And he and Captain Clark's son were lifelong friends.

What became of Sacajawea in later years—the intelligent, shy Indian maiden who made the Lewis and Clark expedition a success? Her whereabouts in later life faded into the foggy mists of unrecorded history. One story goes that she died in the Fort Mandan vicinity a few years after she returned, presumably of a disease or virus unknowingly brought there by white traders. Great respect for her will remain, however. Through pleasantness, honesty, and service, Sacajawea earned the love of Indians and whites alike. Along her trail of no return she proved that Indians were not savages, as many white people at the time believed, but human beings who reacted to friendship or hostility as the occasion presented itself. Today in history Sacajawea lives as a truly remarkable personality of the Great West and is a credit to the North American Indian.

V

The Day Black Hawk Saw Red

With the American revolution an ingenious accomplishment of the recent past, land in the east was rapidly settled by whites. So what happened? They began moving west, onto land governed by Indian tribes, settling "'cordin' to wood 'n' water." Where was this west? It centered in the tall timbers of today's Michigan, Wisconsin, and Minnesota and in the fertile prairies of Iowa, Illinois, and Indiana, where it was said the soil was so potent, planting in it could be dangerous. Drop a seed and jump back, so the story went. Using a simile of the frontier, whites were moving to the territory "like a spot of raccoon grease on a blanket."

One man in the West who sat uninhibited in the saddle of life was Col. Henry Dodge, a dynamic leader directing the dogmatic miners working the lead mines in southwest Wisconsin and northwest Illinois. Breathed there no man with greater determination! Six feet tall, hard as the head of an Indian tomahawk, courageous, pugnacious, and aggressive, Dodge was a willing fighter. Just his handshake was enough to rattle your molars! When a jury indicted him as a henchman of Aaron Burr, he beat up four jurors and the rest hurriedly reconsidered the verdict and cleared him. Of course he couldn't walk on water, though some of his partisans weren't so sure. But Dodge typified the fiercely independent breed of tough white settlers the Indians faced. When the government threatened to use troops to evict him from Indian land, as daring as a Mississippi riverboat gambler, he rifled his counter challenge: "Let the troopers march! With my miners[1] I can whip all the lazy army regulars at

---

[1]"My miners" were rough and ready frontier bachelors from Missouri, the Carolinas, Virginia, and Georgia mostly, who paddled up the Mississippi River in the 1820s powered by a taste for wealth and adventure. They dug lead from hillsides with pick and shovel. When foul weather overtook them in late autumn, they carved a hole in a hillside, never much larger than ten by twelve feet, with two men living together—enjoying the winter with such luxuries

BLACK HAWK'S RETREAT – 1832

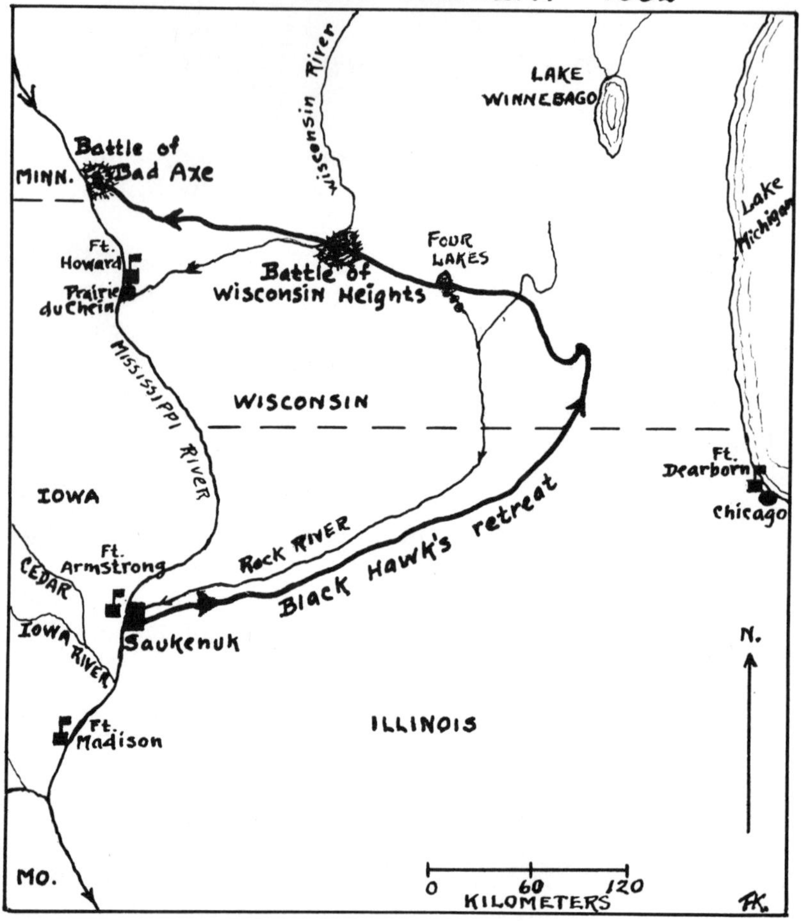

Fort Crawford."[2] Dodge was a man the army loved to hate. Belligerent and fearless, the frontiersman was influenced neither by the rights of the Indian nor by statutory law.

White settlement in the lead mine region had a language all its own and began well ahead of signed treaties with the Indians. Sac and Fox Indians lived on the land for generations, having taken it from the Illinois tribe when the latter was fighting the Potawatomi and Miami for the fertile prairies south of Lake Michigan.

Also called Sauk, the Sac tribe was connected in history with the Fox, whose troubles with Indian neighbors at their earlier homeland they shared. Fighting relentlessly against heavy odds to hold the rich rice fields at Lake Superior, by 1650 the warrior forces of the two tribes had decreased to the point where they were forced southward.

With the Indians settling on land presently occupied by the city of Rock Island, Illinois, Saukenuk became the principal village of their new homeland, which included northwest Illinois and southwest Wisconsin. Trouble with the whites here began early. "Push the Indians out—maybe west of the Mississippi," was the cry of white settlers. The Indians soon learned that sometimes the best deals you make are the ones you don't make. Pressure applied by the United States government forced chiefs of a few small bands to move to Iowa, but some influential chiefs of the tribes vehemently objected. This disagreement between Indians and government became a time bomb. When it burst, the Black Hawk War of 1832 exploded.

Chief Black Hawk was determined to hold land the tribe considered sacred. Born at Saukenuk in 1767, called Makataimeshekiakiak in Sac tongue, he was raised in pleasant surroundings. By birth a Potawatomi, adopted by Sacs, Black Hawk remembered his boyhood well. He loved the prairie and the woods, where he practiced with bow and arrow. Deer, sleek in russet coats, bounced through surreal scenery. A covey of grouse exploded into view. Male cardinals voiced their mating song from treetops. Oak leaves the size of squirrels' ears he saw cautiously unfurling, not

---

as stove, crude chairs, and table. When spring sprung, digging was renewed. Lead mining continued vigorously until news of the California Gold rush reached them, when most miners quickly disappeared.
[2] Fort Crawford at Prairie du Chien, Wisconsin.

trusting the weather. Blossoms on blackberry and gooseberry bushes were forming, while hawthorns and black locusts were proud of their fragrant flowers. With steps as lithe as a panther, he found the greens of spring as soft as cushions. Hepaticas conquered a hilltop, showing like blue sparks struck from the sky. Bloodroots at the base of an oak clasped their leaves around their stems as if huddling from the morning chill. A chipmunk, fat and sassy, scampered, tail erect, along a fallen tree trunk. Violets, blue, pushed their fragile heads through the good earth. The first crop of cottontails ventured from furry nests in the sod. A prairie chicken flashed from a clearing in the woods. Young Black Hawk parted the grass and counted eleven eggs. What a wise mother to nest under the crown of a towering oak where neither hawk nor crow could look from the sky and find their dinner. There was no end to the exciting life of young Black Hawk. He encountered many happenings during his boyhood—including the time he was far from home practicing with bow and arrow when a deafening roar struck him. The noise approaching sounded like several thunder blasts rolled into one. On and on the roar came. Was it a tornado? Black Hawk, taught to lie in a ravine when a tornado approached, looked for a protective gully. Then the noise suddenly was there. Birds! Passenger pigeons by the thousands on their spring flight northward. At first a few blitzed past as fast as light it seemed; the leaders, closely followed by the main body, flying impossibly low. Sun was hidden; momentarily it was dark as night. Black Hawk's ears rang from the roar.

Swift as an arrow the pigeons came—on and on. Was there no end? They darted under, over, and between the prairieland bur oaks. Suddenly, as quickly as they came, they were gone like a thought, carrying the uncontrollable roar with them. They were en route northward on their annual pilgrimage to nesting sites on jackpine trees in central Wisconsin.

Young Black Hawk also learned a thing or two from the graceful killdeer. When unknowingly he approached its ground nest, mother bird moved off unnoticed, then ran upright a few feet—just far enough to catch his eye. Then and there he witnessed a performance worthy of a virtuoso—mother killdeer's mournful call, her quivering wing, her feigned injury. In his innocence, he tried to catch the poor bird to nurse it back to health. Somehow it always flapped itself a step or two out of his reach. Then, when well away from the nest, and much to Black Hawk's surprise, she flew away. Little did he know that the perfectly healthy bird would circle back to her nest. He had succumbed to instinctive trickery by a mistress of the art of subterfuge. Inasmuch as mother killdeer usually chooses open, unprotected places as gravel or bare soil for their nests they distract potential nest robbers by running, feigning a broken wing.

Even before Black Hawk reached manhood, white settlers knew him well—though not as a friend. An understandable hatred fired his heart. Athletic, of medium build, he looked like a creation of the Roman god Mars. His sharp hazel eyes peered past a Roman nose. Only a scalplock adorned his otherwise bald head, as he had removed the remaining hair with clamshell tweezers. His complexion bore a light yellow cast, suggesting an Asian inheritance. His step, soft as a baby's breath, was light and elastic. His eyes were vigilant and alert, his mouth firm. He knew no merit greater than bearing pain without complaint—a strict adherence to Sac teachings. He wore close-fitting "leggins" of deerskin. Elkskin moccasins complemented his small feet, which toed in slightly.

At Saukenuk village, Sac women tilled acres of maize, a tribal food of excellence that they grew in surplus and traded with northern tribes. Beans, tomatoes, squashes, pumpkins, and other fruits and vegetables were grown. Wild apples, plums, cherries, berries, and nuts enhanced the Indian's more than adequate diet. And freeflowing, clear-water springs provided a supreme location for the the Sac village.

In springtime women collected maple tree sap, then boiled it down into syrup and sugar. Legend says that in centuries past, maple syrup was discovered during a disagreement between squaw and brave. Sent by his mate to bring water one evening in early spring, the disgruntled brave abandoned the clay pot at the trunk of a maple tree nearby. Being asked to do "squaw work" was just too much! Venting his wrath, he drove his stone tomahawk into the tree's trunk. Finding the pot filled the next morning, the squaw thought she had been too harsh with her brave. He did bring the water. At least, so she thought. Vension boiled in the liquid had a pleasing flavor.

Knowing something was amiss, the brave decided to investigate. He hadn't brought the water. He was still a warrior—not a squaw! Along the tree trunk he found a liquid dripping from the tree wound. Gathering another pot of sap and boiling it down to a small amount, without the meat, the two made the first maple syrup.

And centuries later whites learned from the Indians the art of making maple syrup and candy.

Though Indians of the southern plains at this time had horses, having acquired them from Mexicans by fair means or foul, tribesmen of this north country had few horses if any. Streams and lakes were Indian highways. On them they paddled dugouts hewn from walnut or butternut tree trunks or lightweight canoes fashioned from birchbark. Overland, afoot, they traveled well-used trails. But every trail required marking, so it could be followed through the wilderness. Sometimes the top of a young tree was tied partially down, pointing the direction of the trail; othertimes a sapling was fractionally broken, signaling the way. Thereafter, these grew into sizable trees, their trunks for decades pointing along the trail.

Prairieland bordering Saukenuk abounded with wildlife. Bison were many, great herds in season fed on prairie grass shoulder-high to a man. Prairie chickens were everywhere. Swans, geese, and ducks found waterways and wetlands to their liking. There were broods of blue-winged teal, some just completing flight training—twisting, turning, diving down for splash landings—and fledglings who had already won their wings. Passenger pigeons, great flocks,

Timber wolf—big game hunter without equal.

Courtesy of the Wisconsin Department of Natural Resources.

passed through. Deer, prime and fat, roamed the woods. Elk abounded in woodland openings. Wild turkeys, alert, gobbled in the bluffs along the river.

Saukenuk, containing more than a hundred lodges, gave an impression of neatness and order—unusual for Indian habitations. Sacs particularly reflected this pride of appearance—even in their dress. But each lodge, roughly fifty feet long and twenty feet wide, was built for shelter, surely not warmth. To the Indians, however, the structures served them well. Sides of the lodges were covered with bark, tops with buffalo hides. Each lodge housed more than one family. Inside, log benches along the side walls were covered with tanned bearskin or buckskin. In the lodge's center was space for an open fire—the sole heating unit for the large structure and the only place to cook food. Smoke escaped through a small hole at the top but too often it lost its way and never found the hole. During heavy weather, the smoke cloud hung in the lodge to the point where a member of the family could hardly recognize kinfolk across the room. But it did keep mosquitos and other insect pests at bay. Outside the lodges, on fences made of poles laced with branches, squash and melon vines trailed, segregating the space into compartments—giving families a certain degree of privacy.

During periods of plenty, gaiety through feasting and dancing abounded in the village. Footraces were run, ball games played. With fifty warriors engaged in a game of lacrosse on the open prairie against another tribe, the game oftentimes looked like gang warfare! Armed with wooden rackets and in more recent years electrified with a drink brought in by white traders, the participants turned the violent sport into a modified form of mayhem. Such an obstreperous game today would require more paramedics than participants.

Take running in comparatively modern times! No chance for Indians to compete with whites in athletic contests until 1912 when Jim Thorpe came along. A young Sac attending the Carlisle Indian School, Thorpe, with some misgivings, tried out for the United States Olympic track team. Unaccountably, the United States permitted him to compete in this prestigious event against the best track men of the world. And Thorpe became the talk of the Olympics after winning gold medals for the United States in both the decathlon and pentathlon, an achievement never before accomplished by any nation. Now back to Black Hawk!

Of the Sacs and Foxes, the Sacs especially were highly respected for their fighting ability. Growing to manhood with a nourishing diet, having adequate exercise, and loving the out of doors contributed to the Sac brave's fine physique. Attired in breechclout, moccasions, adorned with multicolored porcupine-quill trimmings, scalplock covered with vermillion, face streaked with yellow, red, and blue, a strand of bear's claws around his neck with earrings to match, the young Sac brave was indeed a grandiose sight.

From Saukenuk the Indians fanned out in all directions to trap beaver, otter, and other animals enclosed in quality fur. Prior to the War of 1812, the pelts were sold to traders representing European nations. After the war, and profiting from Congress's exclusion of foreigners from the Indian trade, John Jacob Astor's American Fur Company enjoyed a virtual monopoly of the thriving Sac and Fox fur business. Lewis and Clark in 1806 paid both tribes a splendid compliment when they publicly announced that these Indians were the best trappers and hunters in the Upper Mississippi Region.

Monumental problems soon developed, however. Transactions between the Indians and traders involved credit, and, even worse, the Indians seemed to run behind with their payments. But this arrangment, for a time at least, satisfied the trader who felt he had a stranglehold on tribe business. Pelts warriors obtained during winter repaid their debts for the previous spring. Then the following autumn each Indian again was outfitted with traps and supplied

Delivering furs by birchbark canoe.

on credit. Additional purchases, again on credit, were made throughout the winter, and if one follows the trader's usually weighted records, the pelts supplied by the Indian failed to pay the debt owed. Treaties at the time between the Indians and the United States government were being initiated. So what did the fur company do? It had the debt written into the treaty the government made with the two tribes. First the fur company was paid the amount it claimed the Indian trappers were in arrears—the tribe received the remainder, oftentimes nothing.

Fortunately, the government at first relied primarily on its Indian agents to deal with Indian tribes. Though political appointees mostly, Indian agents usually were white men of repute and able representatives of the nation's interests in this Old Northwest Territory. It was a sad day for Indians and government when the military took over.

Fox Indians, though fierce fighters, failed to enjoy the prestige accorded the Sacs. Being constantly at war over the years, particularly when living near Lake Superior, took its toll. In 1804 at Saukenuk they numbered less than two thousand, compared to about five thousand Sacs. Some of the prestige afforded the Sacs was due to the effective political organization of the tribe, something in which the Fox Indians were less efficient.

The Sac tribe had several civil chiefs, with one given top rank—war chief. But only when wise in council and brave on field of battle did a war chief exert much authority. Even then, an influential chief followed the wishes of the tribal council, consisting primarily of grizzled old members who, during younger years, fought enemies with determination and valor. Thus the war chief ruled only so long as he won over enemy tribes.

Typically, the first love of a Sac brave was war. At age fifteen, Black Hawk already had wounded an enemy warrior in combat—a feat that earned him the right to be called a brave, paint his body, and wear feathers. Thereafter, he was a member of every war party that left Saukenuk to thrash enemies. At age twenty-one, when afforded the honor of war chief, he led the parties.

As war chief, Black Hawk instilled confidence in his warriors, and he himself displayed qualities of balance and toughness. Not only brave, he was shrewd and crafty. His imaginative wizardry consistently outmaneuvered his enemies in battle. After a precisely orchestrated raid on an enemy village, he made the trail of his war

Seeking revenge.

party disappear like a cloud's shadow. How? The foremost warrior, running at top speed, leaped from the trail to one side, alighting softly on his toes. Then he carefully smoothed his landing spot so it looked undisturbed. With the remaining warriors continuing their trot along the trail, the lead man at varying intervals made a similar exit until the entire war party vanished. This disappearing act by Sac and Fox war parties gave enemies fits. After the leap from the trail, each warrior was on his own, en route to Saukenuk village. They were not permitted to assemble and return as a group. But this strategy posed no hardship as young men of the tribes from infancy were taught to thread their way through unfamiliar territory and, when necessary, to live off the land.

Prior to each raid, Black Hawk followed the sacred Sac custom of fasting and praying—communicating with the Great Spirit. Visions of Osage or Sioux warrior enemies oftentimes appeared. A fighting force then was recruited for a war party and Black Hawk personally interviewed each warrior.

But fighting Indian enemies soon was almost forgotten as even more formidable foes appeared on the horizon. White settlers were pushing west, and they came with no invitation onto land the Sac and Fox had held for generations. Trouble brewed! Were they not trespassers? More white settlers! Enemy tribes quickly patched up their differences when settlers began encroaching upon Saukenuk. Whites, backed by the military, now were the enemy.

Disagreements between whites and Indians became more frequent, many totally irreconcilable. In individual cases courts dealt with the guilty parties, white or Indian, and in a few instances compensation for property damage was awarded. But no Indians served on juries. With the prejudice white settlers had against Indians, it was rare indeed when a jury of frontiersmen convicted a white man of any crime against an Indian. Furthermore, Indians were reluctant to appear and testify in court—something totally unreal to tribal beliefs. And when an Indian was charged with a crime, he could not be readily identified and, if identified, located. Thus white man's laws did not solve differences between the frontiersman and the Indian.

From the very beginning Black Hawk opposed the whites, evisioning them an unruly trespassers taking tribal land. Some of his views may have been shaped by misinformation. He was told that whites were few in number, not knowing that whites at the time bore large families and that cities in the east were springing up here, there, and everywhere. But Black Hawk was sure of one thing. He knew that whites could not fight up to Indian standards.

Part of the tragedy of the American Indian at the time lay in his inability to understand white man's lust for land. The settler moved in with preconceived and well-defined ideas about property. Land ownership to him was a civil right guaranteed by the government.

Quite different was the Indian view. Land was held as common property of the tribe—if actually owned at all. It was more the property of nature, borrowed to use discreetly. Land not only provided subsistence; it gave meaning and identity to the Indian's very existence. In a strict sense, he belonged to the land rather than the land belonged to him. Such reasoning to the white man was meaningless. Here was land—much land, the promised land, to be won—and if Indians interfered, they would be dealt with by white man's methods.

Pioneer white settler and his family in their Sunday finest.
Courtesy of the State Historical Society of Wisconsin

Confusion now reigned among the Indians. In 1804 at Saint Louis, Sac and Fox chiefs of a few clans placed a mark on a treaty that would provide the two tribes a government annuity totalling one thousand dollars, but only if they moved to a reservation west of the Mississippi River. Black Hawk, always prudent and cautious, alleged that the chiefs at time of signing were under the influence of a strong beverage furnished by the other party and successfully stopped the transaction.

In 1816, however, a treaty was formulated in which Black Hawk was a party, by white man's laws. But he insisted that he and the other chiefs did not understand white man's customs. "Yes, I touched the goose quill to the paper as they motioned me to do," Black Hawk said afterward, "but they didn't tell me that by this act I consented to give away my village and the land I love." Unfamiliar with white man's ways, the Indians simply did not understand that by placing a mark on the treaty, they agreed to give away their home village Saukenuk and the thousands of acres of land they called home. "Include me out," Black Hawk demanded. Yet the written document prevailed. But some years later the main body of the Sac and Fox tribes, led by Chief Keokuk, did move to a reservation in today's Iowa. Black Hawk refused to go, insisting he did not smoke to the agreement, as per Sac custom, thus there was no treaty.

No sooner was one difficulty at least partially settled than another surfaced. In 1830, chiefs of the Foxes were invited by the government to Prairie du Chien, Wisconsin, to settle their difficulties with the Sioux. En route, Sioux warriors jumped the Fox, killing nine. Obsessed with a burning desire for revenge, the following year within a mile of Prairie du Chien Black Hawk's war party attacked a band of Sioux, killing twenty-eight. A fire-storm of criticism by our government demanded the murderers be handed over but Black Hawk refused. Seeds of discontent skyrocketed into an inferno. To add fuel to the fire, when Black Hawk heard his people would be forcefully evicted from Saukenuk and moved west of the Mississippi if they did not move voluntarily, he chose to oppose the order and became leader of dissidents.

Black Hawk and his band continued living at Saukenuk despite threats from the military. He agreed to release to whites the then active lead mines, if his people could keep their home village. Those who moved west of the Mississippi sent word back that they were there without lodges that had been promised. Uneasiness grew! A few warriors with families returned, determined to repossess their lands. But confusion on the white front also brewed! When Governor Reynolds declared Illinois was invaded by hostile Indians, six companies of regular soldiers and seven hundred militia were ordered out under General Gaines.

But Black Hawk had no intention of making history. He vowed to fight with a fervor beyond comprehension if the military moved to take Saukenuk, being aware that it would be a battle to the death with no promise of tomorrow. Displaying a strong hostility, he said sorrowfully, "We are a divided people now. Keokuk heads one group and is willing to forfeit our rights to those I don't trust. And he is a coward to desert Saukenuk. I head the true band of Sacs and Foxes. Why should we be forced to leave our home and the land the Great Spirit let us use for generations?" Ordered to leave by the military, he sent this message: "We will protect our homes unto death. Our tribe has no right to sell land which belongs to the Great Spirit above!"

By now whites had taken the lead mines. While Keokuk was

at Saint Louis dealing with the government and Black Hawk was away from Saukenuk for a few days, armed white settlers invaded the village and claimed the Indian fields of maize. Keokuk's mission was unsuccessful, as even he figured the government demands were too harsh. When Black Hawk returned to Saukenuk he was ready to spit blood, passionately insisting that Saukenuk had been mortally wounded.

His rancor toward whites bit like a prairie rattler. Still, whites continued their pressure by destroying the maize squaws had planted and cultivated. The usual tranquillity at Saukenuk disappeared faster than a July snowfall!

Black Hawk decided to meet with Winnebago and Potawatomi chiefs, as these tribes were his friends and had agreed to give his band planting ground. In April 1832, they met along Sycamore Creek where it empties into Rock River. Though friendly to Black Hawk's cause, the other chiefs would have no part of his scheme for war. So Black Hawk decided to move his band to Iowa territory, recruit others, then return and fight the military. But during the few days at this camp, Major Stillman's scouts, totalling 270 mounted soldiers, were sent to find Black Hawk and take him prisoner. While dogs were roasting for the evening feast, Black Hawk's sentinels burst into camp having seen in the distance mounted soldiers approaching. These, of course, were Major Stillman's troopers.

Black Hawk's campsite, chosen for entertaining his Winnebago and Potawatomi friends, was anything but a defensive stronghold to fight an enemy. He ordered his people to leave immediately; they headed northward up the Rock River as fast as they could travel afoot. Even then Black Hawk sought a conference with the military leader, sending five warriors with a flag of truce and no guns. Four were shot at sight—the fifth escaped and returned to his chief. With eyes blazing hate, Black Hawk saw red! He now realized the horrendously difficult situation confronting him. It was enough to make his blood curdle. "We must attack and avenge the death of our warriors," Black Hawk agonized, and the war cry erupted! Secreting his women and children in a thicket, he selected a picked group of warriors to ambush the troopers pursuing him. How foxlike was his cunning—how brilliant his planning. Choosing a site he considered proper, Black Hawk hid warriors behind trees and bushes, even the riverbank. Every warrior, it seems, knew well the idiosyncrasies of the others and acted accordingly. When the mounted troops were less than a stone's throw away, warriors from all sides attacked like hungry sharks savagely feeding, using guns, tomahawks, knives, and clubs, yelling the Sac war cry. Horses became so unmanageable and so many troopers were falling that Major Stillman ordered a quick retreat. It soon became a rout. With 70 warriors Black Hawk put to flight a detachment of 270 soldiers, killing several.

In the meantime, other military units were being assembled to fight Black Hawk, who seemed as elusive as a cloud's shadow. General Atkinson organized a force of several hundred soldiers, and before long about three thousand troopers were pursuing Black Hawk's plodding band of five hundred Indians, including old folks, women, and children.

Determined that no help from other Indian tribes came to the Sac and Fox, on May 25, 1832, Gen. Henry Dodge (later territorial governor of Wisconsin) presented this razor-sharp message to Winnebago Indians then encamped on the northwest shore of present-day Lake Mendota: "Your residence being near our settlements, it is necessary and proper that we should explicitly understand you, the chiefs and warriors, whether or not you intend to aid, harbour or counsel the Sacs in your country; to do so will be considered as a declaration of war on your part . . . The Sacs have killed eleven of our people, and wounded three; our people have killed eleven of the Sacs. We have told you the consequences of uniting with our enemies; we hope, forever, that the bright chain of friendship will still continue; that we may travel the same road of friendship, under a clear sky."

Atkinson's force reached Lake Koshkonong in today's southern Wisconsin on July 3. Well ahead of the military, Black Hawk hid his trail at this point, but even then his entourage had no time to stop and smell wild roses. Atkinson lost the Hawk's trail and remained encamped at the lake for five days, trying to locate it. By now General Dodge was pursuing the Indian band with two select brigades of mounted men. Discovering the trail along the Rock River near the location of our present city of Watertown, Dodge gave chase. The trail was fresh and led westward toward Four Lakes—a collective term for First Lake, Second Lake, and so on, First Lake being today's Lake Kegonsa and Fourth Lake Lake Mendota at Madison.

Despite the women and children in the band, catching Black Hawk was no Sunday picnic. His skill as a tactician and ability as a commander were demonstrated by exercising ingenious strategy during his famous flight through the wilds of southern Wisconsin. He moved his people in three divisions. The main body, old folks, women, and children, walked in the center with a division of warriors on each side; thus the center section was shielded from ambuscade or attack from either side by picked warriors walking the right and left wings.

By July 19, the military was in hot pursuit. Mounted men could maintain consistent travel speed. Black Hawk now had no time to cover his trail, as the walking women and children, already fatigued, slowed the pace. That night he encamped between Rock River and Second Lake (Lake Waubesa). The following day the band reached Third Lake (Lake Monona), avoiding the well-known Indian trail along the lakeshore. But the military horsemen were now closing in. When the troopers camped on the east side of Third Lake, the Indians were encamped on the southwest shore of Fourth Lake on today's University of Wisconsin—Madison campus. The high hill south of camp concealed the subdued smoke of their campfires from the military.

On the morning of July 21, 1832, one military force followed Black Hawk's trail over Catfish Creek, today's Yahara River. It led over the knoll on which Wisconsin's state capital rests today. At the location of the abandoned Chicago and Northwestern Railroad depot at South Blair and East Wilson streets, now occupied by a gas and electric company, a lone Indian warrior suffered in silence. Bravely he stood alone on a small mound, the grave of his wife, buried three years earlier. As the military men approached, facing them he opened his buckskin shirt, bared his chest, and waited for the musket charge. The soldiers accommodated him. He lay where he fell. The soldiers hurried on.

In his haste, Black Hawk's trail was becoming clearer. Hard on his heels, the army was gaining fast. From Lake Mendota the trail headed northwest. Following, the mounted soldiers caught up to a proud elderly straggler who became exhausted and fell behind the main body. Shot, as he fell, using the last ounce of strength to discharge his antiquated weapon, he wounded a soldier. Five o'clock that afternoon the military reached the bluffs of the Wisconsin river, a mile south of present-day Sauk City, Wisconsin. From that vantage point soldiers saw the Indian women and children on the east bank of the river readying to cross.

With the instincts of an alley cat, crafty Black Hawk assigned about fifty young warriors to hide in the bluffs and another group of seasoned warriors below to form a second line of defense. They would hold the military column back until the women and children crossed the wide stream. The first columns to reach the bluffs were those of Colonels Dodge and Ewing. Henry's brigade appeared shortly thereafter. Dismounting, the troopers formed a battle line and the fight was on! The ferocity of these Sac and Fox warriors is best explained in an article written by Hon. Saterlee Clark, who took part in the battle, published in volume 8 of *Wisconsin Historical Collections*. He reports: " . . . only about one hundred and twenty half-starved Indians defended the pass against nearly three thousand whites, while the remaining Indians in plain sight were crossing the river with the women and children, and as soon as these were safe the Indians broke and ran."

Called the Battle of Wisconsin Heights, the fight lasted about two hours—just long enough for the Indians at the river to hurriedly fashion rafts of logs, tying the logs together with grapevines, and cross the stream, When they signalled that the crossing was accomplished, warriors at the bluffs broke away. Great swimmers, they crossed the Wisconsin and caught up with the main body plodding along, showing painful signs of exhaustion. Knowing that some extraordinary strategy was necessary to delay the military, Black Hawk segregated his group into small units, then had them fan out so no trail was evident. The units passed stealthily westward through today's Sauk, Richmond, and Crawford counties, with the military attempting to follow individual footprints through the wilderness. The Indians then assembled near the mouth of Bad Axe River where the stream empties into the Mississippi, about forty miles north of Prairie du Chien, Wisconsin—well in advance of the military.

But Black Hawk's band at Bad Axe now totalled only 460 Indians, as some warriors has been killed at Wisconsin Heights and the old who were physically unable to continue the fast pace had wandered quietly from the trail to die in celestial peace. Black Hawk's strategy called for crossing the Mississippi River and reaching Sac and Fox relatives in Iowa Territory. Surely reaching Iowa would end the battle, as it was the location assigned them by the government. But the military didn't want Black Hawk and his band to reach Iowa! It had a new secret weapon on the Mississippi—the armed steamboat *Warrior*.

Arriving at the Mississippi, the Indian women and children began crossing the wide river in any manner possible, and many crossed before the *Warrior*, carrying armed soldiers on board from Fort Crawford, reached the crossing location in midafternoon. How did the women and children cross the wild Mississippi? By holding onto logs or by individually swimming the stream. One mother wrapped her baby in a buckskin hide and held the corners between her teeth while holding the end of a floating log that she steered to the opposite shore.

When the *Warrior* approached the crossing location, it as well as the armed soldiers aboard, opened fire on the women and children in the water. To save them, Black Hawk, still on the Wisconsin shore, despairingly displayed a huge white cloth—a peace offering. It was answered by the *Warrior's* six-pounder cannon. But many women and children already had reached the Iowa shore, where the government ordered them to go, thus thought they were safe. Their freedom was short-lived, as will be reported later.

Cannon and musket fire from the *Warrior* drove Black Hawk and his band on the Wisconsin shore inland toward the approaching militiary units. At this point all hope had been abandoned as it crashed upon the shapeless rocks of reality. On August 2, 1832, this final battle of Black Hawk's war was fought!

If it had not been for the gunboat *Warrior*, a weapon unknown to Black Hawk at the time, the chief's strategy might have succeeded. He almost accomplished a victory that would have been a credit to a military general of any rank. The wily chief stationed a rear guard of twenty warriors to surprise the first military force that arrived, which happened to be Atkinson's, open fire on the troops, then slowly retreat three miles upriver. This action was designed to draw the army away from the women and children, giving them time to cross the Mississippi.

Black Hawk's plan was executed precisely. As Atkinson approached, the twenty warriors from their ambuscade opened fire on the troops, then slowly retreated northward through woods with the military in hot pursuit. The army, thereby, was maneuvered away from the main body of Indians concealed along the shore. Here was a military leader of distinction and reputation being craftily outwitted by an unlettered Indian. Atkinson, and Dodge when he arrived with his troops, both took the bait, but fortunately for the reputation of the military, Colonel Henry, who was doggedly following the dispersed moccasin footprints to the river, correctly interpreted the artful cunning of Black Hawk. Following these to the river instead of bearing northward upriver, he immediately opened fire on the Indian band. Meanwhile, Atkinson and Dodge, hearing heavy firing downstream, discovered they had been misled by a ruse and returned to join the battle.

　　After a suicidal confrontation lasting two hours, the remnants of the twenty warriors returned to defend the women and children. Driven to the river by the military force, Black Hawk's exhausted warriors, now out of ammunition, were shot to pieces by the gunboat from the front and military from the rear. The flag of truce, openly displayed along the Mississippi river bank, was shot down by the *Warrior's* Captain Throckmorton. Here was a brutal act, perhaps unprecedented and unparalleled in the history of honorable warfare. Yet it was second-rate to an even more brutal act that followed.

　　No sooner had the battle ended on the Wisconsin side of the Mississippi when ninety Sioux warriors, bitter enemies of the Sac and Fox, led by Chief Little Crow, took charge on the Iowa side. Prearranged by the military, they massacred in cold blood all the Indian women and children who had crossed to the Iowa shore during Black Hawk's holding action. And they were killed on land west of the Mississippi, the exact territory assigned them by the government. Were it not reported by authorities on the Black Hawk War, and Black Hawk himself after the battle, people of this day would hardly believe that such a brutal act would be permitted.

　　It so happened that this Chief Little Crow was the father of the Sioux chief who at a later date led his vicious band to massacre white settlers in southwestern Minnesota in 1862. Is it possible the son followed in the footsteps of his father and performed an act apparently condoned by the United States military some thirty years earlier?

Despite the cordon of military men surrounding the vanishing Sac and Fox assemblage on the Wisconsin side of the Mississippi, skillful Black Hawk and a few warriors escaped and took refuge with friendly Winnebagos in the Wisconsin Dells vicinity. But this bloody battle at Bad Axe ended the war. In deep sorrow, Black Hawk decided to give himself up. Two young Winnebagos escorted him to Fort Crawford at Prairie Du Chien on August 27, 1832. Dressed in a new white bucksin suit made by Winnebago squaws, Black Hawk stepped bravely forward and related his feelings to the commander: "You have taken me prisoner. I am grieved. I tried to bring you into ambush, but you were too many. Your loaded guns were well aimed. I saw my evil day was at hand. Black Hawk's heart is now dead, but he can take torture. I am no coward. I fought for my people against those who came to cheat us. You know the cause of this war, and you should be ashamed. We believe in the Great Spirit. Farewell—my nation!"

Black Hawk now was sixty-five years old. His two sons, Prophet and Naopope, fiercely loyal to their father, miraculously survived the battle at Bad Axe and eluded capture by the military, although their wives and children who successfully crossed the Mississippi to the Iowa side apparently were murdered. The sons, who also surrendered, and five additional influential warriors were held as hostages at Jefferson Barracks, a military army post near Saint Louis, Missouri.

A prisoner of honor, Black Hawk displayed, as always, impeccable integrity. Even in sorrow his disposition was amiable. No chief by birth, he had acquired his position through sheer bravery, wisdom, and loyalty. During the meeting with President Jackson he said with true dignity, "I am a man; you are another. If I had not struck for my people, they would say I was a woman. Chief Black Hawk expects to return to his people!" Deeply moved by his sincerity, the president commanded the broken chief to Fort Monroe, Virginia, and assured him he eventually would be permitted to rejoin his people in Iowa.

During the next meeting with President Jackson, on June 5, 1833, Black Hawk, his sons, and other warriors held hostage were set free. The chief was first taken on a yawn-provoking trip to the

Seneca Indians's "model reservation" in New York State to observe their mode of living, but he returned unimpressed. Large crowds greeted him along the way—some viewing him a hero, others as an enemy. Taken to Iowa in August, he was met by his people among cheers and drum music. But Keokuk now was the designated chief of the Sacs and Foxes and was accepted by the government. This change drained Black Hawk's authority as a break in a dam destroys a beaver colony. He quietly but firmly refused to accept Keokuk as chief, seeing him as one who had turned traitor and sided with the government. He departed in silence—downcast and broken. Despite the hardship of war—a prisoner for almost a year and broken of his chieftain rank—Black Hawk remained an Indian of magnificent physique, although his fame, like the fame of most heroes, had dimmed with time. He closed one door and opened another, which led to nothing more than a cavalcade of memories.

Withering like a cut flower, Black Hawk spent his last years quietly with his faithful wife and loyal sons on the banks of the Des Moines River in today's Davis County, Iowa. On October 3, 1838, he died and was buried within a mile of his home—near Eldon, Iowa. Dressed in the military uniform presented earlier by President Jackson and the sword given him at the same time, as per Sac custom, his body was seated in the grave. Medals from Jackson, John Quincy Adams, and the city of Boston, which he richly prized, were attached to his uniform. The embellished cane Henry Clay gave him was placed between his knees, grasped by both hands. Then the body was carefully covered with pieces of wood and soil, and, again following Sac custom, its only marker was a mound of earth covering the grave.

But the body of this dynamic Indian leader was denied its final resting place. Medals, sword, and cane was stolen by relic seekers within a year. Even the body was removed and taken to Saint Louis, Missouri, thence to Quincy, Illinois. Complaints by Black Hawk's sons to Governor Lucas of Iowa Territory initiated action that returned the corpse to Iowa, but no relics came back. Black Hawk's bones were placed in the Burlington Geological and Historical Society Building at Burlington, Iowa, where they burned along with the building in 1855.

In Black Hawk's honor, a huge statue personifying him, fashioned by the famous sculptor Lorado Taft, stands on a high buff near Oregon, Illinois, overlooking the Rock River countryside—land so dear to the noble chief.

These fitting lines by poet Bryant profoundly portray the melancholy ending of Chief Black Hawk and his people:

> A noble race! But they are gone,
> > With their old forests wide and deep,
> And we have built our homes upon
> > Fields where their generations sleep
> Their fountains slake our thirst at noon,
> > Upon their fields our harvest waves,
> Our lovers woo beneath their moon—
> > Oh, let us spare, at least, their graves.

VI

How a Chief Is Made

He happened on a cold day in March 1831. Born on the south bank of Grand River near the present village of Bullhead, South Dakota, this was no ordinary child. He came from intelligent Sioux ancestry—and a family of fighters! He was the only son of his parents, and because Sioux believe a son is the greatest gift of all, this child was especially welcome.

At the time, no one except the mother and father perhaps could foresee the fame he would receive in later life, and at times they too had their doubts about his future. He was a child with extraordinary determination. As an infant, unlike others his age, he was disgustingly deliberate. As a result he began life with no better affectionate name than Slow. Given food to eat, he held it in his tiny hand, examined it carefully, and turned it over at least once before making up his mind to eat it. Once it was accepted, no one could take it from him.

The mother took good care of her son. Strapped to a baby-board attached to the side of her bison-hide saddle, he bounced with the rhythmic steps of the pony, viewing the ever-changing countryside. When a bit older, tucked inside soft buckskin attached to his mother's shoulders and over her back, nose and eyes barely visible, he looked into the azure sky. When still older, he rode in a basket on a travois just above the spot where the two lodgepoles dragging on the ground crossed, somewhat above the pony's withers. Sitting in restrained comfort behind the pony's tail, his small hands holding fast when the pony trotted, he watched as the endless field of prairie grass slid under his basket. Crossing streams, he closed his eyes and held his breath as water splashed against his face. When five winters old, he rode atop the pony behind his mother, holding firmly to her buckskin belt, his short legs pointed straight out. At ten he seemed to live on his own pony, his growing legs shaping themselves to the curved body of the animal, making him bowlegged for life.

Slow had a happy childhood. Still, he displayed a certain awkwardness when he moved his sturdy body inasmuch as his movements were meticulously deliberate. Unlike other boys, he would never proceed before thinking the matter through. But he was a strong, lively Indian boy and found the world exactly made for him. Were not the Sioux (Dakota) the greatest? Was not his tribe, the Hunkpapa, the bravest of all? Were not the Hunkpapa warriors victorious on every front? Did they not keep enemy tribes from their rich domain? Didn't the Hunkpapa hold the heart of the bison lands and the luxuriant woods along streams? Weren't the Sioux hunting grounds so vast his people were constantly on the move, leisurely making camp here, there, and everywhere, following the great bison herds?

Something always was happening on the prairie. In early spring pasque flowers pushed their heads through the productive soil, coloring the landscape an exquisite soft purple. Trees on stream bottomland opened up their hearts, displaying colors of inviting shades of green. The grass was an emerald hue, while pussy willows adorned willow and cottonwood trees along waterways. And so the natural life of the country was with him. He understood that the countryside did not depend on the Crow or the Blackfeet or even the Sioux. It was independent of all. In springtime, nature was at its unmitigated best!

Slow soon learned that even without the Indian, the prairie had a life all its own, displaying beauty, spirit, vitality. Despite one tribe hostile to another, the Sioux lived their own lives, forming a healthy self-sustaining family, like nature itself in springtime. The future was gloriously inspirational on the great open spaces. Crops were building for the autumn. Crops? Yes, bison!

How Slow liked the constant travel from one campsite to another, seeing the world—learning. While the dawn prairieland came to life, he rounded up the family ponies (yes, his father Jumping Bull was considered wealthy by Indian standards, owning several fine horses); he enjoyed the responsibility given him. Each morning, as per Sioux custom, Jumping Bull stepped from his tepee, faced the source of all life, the rising sun, and stood in silence for a few moments before becoming enmeshed in the day's activities. The son dreamed he would do likewise and soon would be given a stronger bow and a quiver of stone-pointed arrows. Shivering with anticipation, the boy's heart beat with pride as he envisioned an exciting future.

Slow's feet longed to touch the ground and take off, stealing forth in moccasined silence. His fingers itched to grasp the strong bow and needle-sharp stone-tipped arrows. With dark brown eyes as bright as a captive birds, they were eager to squint and take aim. He worked diligently to reach the zenith of accomplishment perfection. His heart was set to learn the rewarding language of the land. As a budding warrior, understandably he taught himself not to fear the sounds of the prairie, nor those in the woods at night. Being completely alone did not frighten him. He knew that if one really knows nature, its very silence speaks to him.

While Slow rounded up the ponies for their move to another campsite, his mother took down the tepee, mindfully folding the bison hides and piling them alongside the lodgepoles. Bright sunshine showed the gentle part of the day. One by one, family tepees came down. Poles, bison hides tied together with rawhide strips, robes, implements and stone tools were spread over the ground in orderly confusion. Shaggy packhorses stood impatiently while tepee poles were lashed to their sides and packs of luggage tied upon travois behind them. Jumping on top, women and children rode away on the huge bundles. Slow did likewise! How much fun he had looking this way and that, watching the wolflike dogs, their red tongues hanging between two sets of sharp white teeth, their heavy packs keeping them tired and in the march column. How he enjoyed watching the colts, young like him, running about, the herd of loose ponies being kept in line by men on fine horses, the parading of warriors adorned in eagle feathers riding the flanks, carrying a bow and many arrows in their quivers. He saw the long lance under each warrior's leg on the side of his horse, ready for any emergency.

It was a busy life of action for Slow, determined to excel at every opportunity. Yet he envisioned his responsibilities as few—rising early, caring for the family ponies, hunting small game for food with bow and blunt arrows, testing his accuracy at every draw. There were foot races to be run, pony races, bow and arrow contests, hurling the lance for accuracy and distance, wrestling, and swimming. Thankful he was that the future came only one day at a time, thus the distant tomorrows most likely would take care of themselves.

Arriving at the new camp location, packs unloaded, he set his father's ponies out to graze, hobbling the front feet of the leader to keep them from wondering away. Tepees rose like colorful crocuses in early spring, each at a designated location according to the family status in the tribe. How sweet the smell of food cooking, soup in the kettle, meat broiling over the flame! Then the enjoyment of eating—crisp white tipsin, tart cherries and berries, and hot food. No one else, he as sure, ate so well! After darkness, around a small fire in his family tepee, he was put to sleep listening to the exciting experiences of Sioux heroes, their superior bravery, their daring raids on enemies. Prestige to a warrior, he concluded, is all-important, won only in battle. (Neither white settlers nor the military had interfered with the Sioux thus far.) At times the boy awakens in his sleep, dreams of the day he will become a proud warrior—brave and honored. Thus far his status is no higher than that of a squaw. Humiliating!

But Slow is continually being taught by his understanding father not to be a bully, yet to permit no one to throw sand in his face either! At irregular times the father attempts to frighten his son during the night by shouting a Crow war whoop. A model of consistency, the boy throws off his bison-robe blanket, springs to his feet, seizes his bow and arrows with needle-sharp stone points that he is permitted to use in self-defense, and is ready to battle the enemy. In this manner the father is training his young son to defend the Sioux camp during a surprise night attack.

War, day or night, was a constant unfriendly companion. It came as surely as the sun rose gold in the east. Even when Slow was a baby, his mother put her son to bed in tiny moccasins she made, knowing that an enemy could attack the camp any night and force the women to run and hide their children in the darkness. Children as infants were taught never to cry, as the sound would disclose the location of their hiding place. The penalty for crying was severe—breathing parts of the anatomy completely covered until crying ceased. During an enemy attack the mother held a hand over her baby's nose and mouth, barely permitting breathing. At the slightest whimper, oxygen was cut off even to the point where the baby would turn limp and die in the mother's arms. But in the quiet of camp, babies were taught not to cry—if they did so, the rule was strict: no air to breathe. A baby soon got the message—crying was not for him or her!

Slow at nightime was taught to fear any unnatural hoot of the owl—used by enemies to signal an attack. Small boys, tomorrow's warriors, were especially vulnerable to bashed heads by blows from enemy tomahawks. Being ten winters old, Slow was taught to stand and fight with the men and be brave. And he was coached not to fear an honorable death in battle, to take injury gracefully, and to contribute his rightful share so the Hunkpapa could stage their victory dance. Didn't Slow's uncle die in glory on the field of battle only a few moons ago? And when he no longer could sit his pony, when blood loss was draining his life, didn't he admit no injury? Asked by a sympathetic warrior kneeling over him, "Where did you get hit?" he replied with no reference to his severe wound, "Over there," pointing to a knoll a half-mile away.

Warfare had top priority in the life of a Sioux, but the time expended on this activity ran second to that of making a living. First, the Sioux were bison hunters. Its flesh was their principal food, its hide was made into tepees, clothing, bed mats, blankets, bullboats to cross streams and sacks in which personal luggage was packed. Into clean bison intestines was stuffed pemmican—made from bison meat, berries, and suet. Sinews from the animal made bowstrings; thread, when braided, rope; blood made paint; hooves, gave the Sioux glue; bones were carved into utensils and implements. Bison hair was plugged into soft buckskin pillows and packed into saddle seats, tallow mixed with ochre painted Sioux faces, dung was used for fuel, and horn was shaped into weapons and carved into cups, knives, spoons, and ornaments.

Without bison the Indian of the plains and prairie was helpless, inasmuch as these people lived and died with the bison. Their civilization rested squarely upon its broad shoulders, before and after white man's horse came to the Indian as a new means of transport. Though white man today thinks much like the Sioux years earlier, his thoughts are different. He thinks about machines—yes, machines—and the person who can diligently operate one is considered the most successful. The Indian thought "bison"—how to produce useful products from these shaggy bovines. But unlike

Courtesy of the Milwaukee Public Museum.

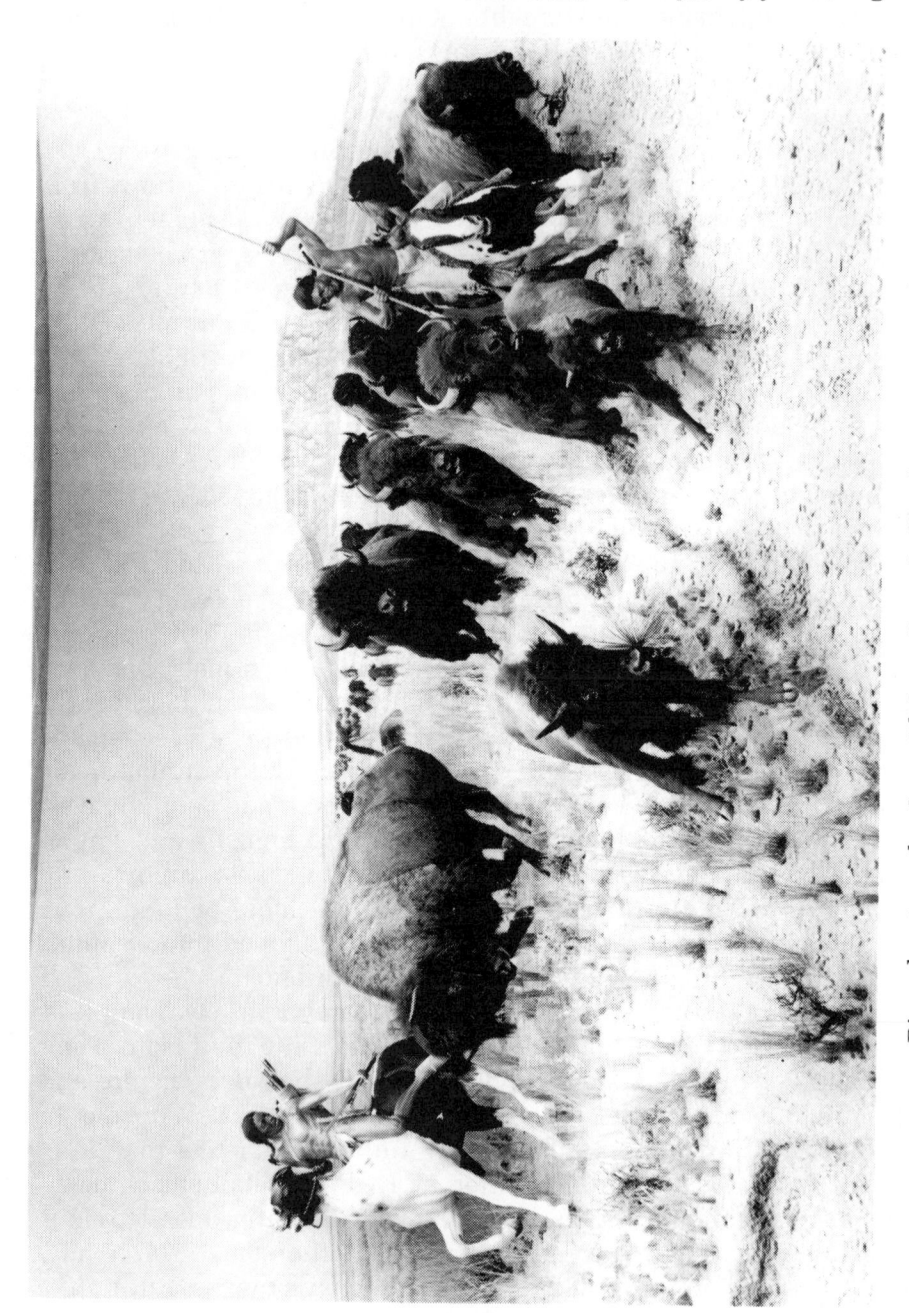

Bison hunt on the Great Plains—Crow Indian hunters on swift pinto ponies stampede herd and choose choice animals for food, lodges, clothing, and implements.

white man at a later date, the Indian never exploited the animal and killed only the number needed to sustain him—no more!

Slow, though of average height for his years, grew into a radiant young man with shoulders strong as the jaws of a prairie wolf. Humble but confident, he was the type of leader young men admired. He became extraordinarily skillful with the bow and arrow. His powerful physique helped him throw the lance an unbelievable distance. He realized no award was achieved through mediocrity and that pursuit of excellence required compelling sacrifices. So he felt he must drive himself to the artistic trajectory of perfection. Four winters back he killed his first bison. Bravery he displayed on many occasions. When an enemy warrior was caught casing the camp one night and killed, the body was dragged into the circle of tepees. After cautious deliberation, the boy came forward and touched the bloody image of death. Being the first boy volunteering to do so labeled him the bravest youth in camp.

But Slow's studied calculations—his method of thinking through every detail like a general planning a military campaign concerned the father. Still, he gave his son the fleetest horse, probably the swiftest of all ponies in camp, and counseled him. "The man most successful is he who is foremost. On the hunt or in war, the man who is foremost has the fastest horse. My son, you must be foremost and brave! Here—here is a coup-stick I made for you to strike the enemy." Thus the father gave his son a depth of faith that unmistakably showed!

The coup-stick was an arm-long peeled wand with a feather tied to the small end, Striking a live human enemy with the stick was known as a coup. This deed was ranked far above killing an enemy warrior. Horses stolen, weapons acquired, and rescues of wounded comrades also counted for honors, but the coup was the greatest honor of all. Judged on this basis, the goal of a Sioux warrior was aimed at winning coups, thus achieving a high rank in the tribe and the many social privileges accompanying it. In a spirited race toward the enemy you were fighting, the first Sioux could attain the coveted honor of a coup and let laggards make the kill—an honor of lesser rank. As the warrior struck the enemy with a coup-stick, he shouted his name so he would have witnesses to his deed. When the warriors assembled after the battle, each claimed the deed to which he was entitled. Having one or more witnesses, he was permitted to narrate his feat before other members of the warrior society—in fact, he was forced to do so before he could take credit for the coup. Penalties were imposed on those who tried to take credit for a coup without actually accomplishing the deed, and, in cases of great magnitude, the warrior was placed in such disgrace he was not even permitted to name his own children. In severe instances the warrior was removed from membership in the tribe and forced to leave camp, a disgrace so serious it suggested suicide.

Warfare on the prairies and plains, as performed by Indians on horseback, was perhaps the greatest and most dangerous sport the world has known. Any red-blooded sportsman of this day who loves horses surely would thrill at such turbulent sporting chances. It carried the excitement of a fox hunt, the dangers of hunting the wild boar, the dash of horse polo, and the exciting chance of a horse race, with more than enough dangers to satisfy the most reckless. But believe me—this type of game was only for the proficient and brave, as Indians seldom gave, nor did they expect, quarter.

Yet the Sioux made war a fight of grandstand plays—seeking coups for the most part, save in instances of revenge or protecting family and tribe. The prime purpose was to distinguish himself rather than to destroy his enemy. Before the horse, hand-to-hand combat was the only form of warfare, simply because the warrior had no fast means of movement nor long-range weapons. With the introduction of the horse, warfare—man against man on horse—became the finest art. The bravest warriors were willing to take mounmental risks to strike the enemy with a coup-stick, or the feathered end of an arrow if they had no coup-stick with them, rather than shoot him down. They realized this was sport of the highest risk and the greatest reward. Public honor, social prestige, and wealth were the top prizes. But the combatant who distinguished himself in battle and fell died honorably and was given his reward with due ceremony.

One day in the busy life of Slow, Hunkpapa scouts, always watching the distant horizon, excitedly reported the sight of an enemy war party advancing toward their camp. Hidden behind a low ridge, Sioux scouts kept watch. In camp the call for battle was sounded by soft, rapid beating of drums. A small group of chosen warriors assembled and cautiously advanced under the direction of the chief. The head scout at a selected location leaped from his pony and, kneeling, hastily pulled up a handful of prairie grass. Using it as a camouflage, he peered over the ridge top. Watching the advance of the unsuspecting Crow enemy, he signaled their approach while the anxious Sioux warriors prepared for battle. Bows, pulled from quivers, were hurriedly strung and tested. Arrows were arranged in quivers for quick grasp. Warriors with lances uncovered their shields. The trap was set.

Closer and closer the Crows came, with the Sioux anxiously waiting for the signal to charge over the ridge. All eyes were riveted on the chief. Just as the attack signal was given, a boy in war paint, mounted on a gray pony, suddenly appeared from nowhere. Seeing the signal, he charged. With pony already going at full speed, he had a running start. Over the rise, off like a wind-driven prairie fire he went, with Sioux warriors following. Clothed only in breechcloth and moccasins, he held his coup-stick high. His fleet mount, carrying less weight than a grown warrior, outdistanced the others. Here was the chance the boy had dreamed about. Wrapping his legs around the pony's belly, he shouted the fierce Sioux war cry.

As the Sioux charged over the ridge, they drew a moment's hestitation from the Crow warriors. Surprised, the chief was forced to make a quick decision. Should they meet the Sioux in open combat, the Crow chief pondered. How large a force was hidden over the rise? Was it a Sioux trap? Would this Sioux force engage them in battle, others concealed over the ridge surround and annihilate his Crow war party? The decision was made! The Crow chief would not take the risk! Wheeling his pony in its tracks, he sped away as fast as the mount could carry him, the other Crows following. But the Sioux war cry was coming closer and closer. Crows on the slower mounts were in danger. Using quirts freely, both tribes strained their ponies to the limit.

But how about the boy rider? Who was he? And from where did he come? The Sioux chief leading the charge thought he resembled Slow, Jumping Bull's son. He was now well ahead of the Sioux warriors and the chief. Soon he was breathing down the back of the hindmost Crow. Hearing pounding hooves approaching closer and closer, the Crow chose to end his life in glory. Leaping from his mount, bow and arrow in hand, he set himself to drive an arrow through his pursuer.

It was common knowledge among those who fought plains

Indians that the most daring were the young men. They took grave chances, sometimes foolhardy ones. Here, instead of the boy propelling himself to the opposite side of his mount and racing past as an experienced warrior might do to avoid the arrow, he kept his pony going straight at the Crow. He was out to win honor, not run from it. He was aiming for a coup—his first coup—or else he would lie prostrate on the battlefield and achieve honors posthumously. As the boy put his face against the pony's mane, the mount charged the warrior. Raising his head as he reached the enemy, the boy quickly struck the wrist of the warrior with his coup-stick, spoiling the Crow's aim. Swish! The arrow missed its mark! At the same time the boy yelled, "I, Slow, have won over you!" as the pony brushed the enemy down. A Sioux warrior following drove a lance through the Crow before he could rise to set another arrow.

When the running battle terminated, many Crow warriors lay on the battlefield. The Sioux chief did not press the point and called off the chase. There was no need to kill more Crows, as it was a battle the enemy would not soon forget. The Hunkpapa even surprised themselves—they fought like men possessed—inspired by a courageous and daring boy too young to have his own long bow and sharp stone-tipped arrows. He had only a coup-stick!

Yet the chief approached the lad with misgivings. Hadn't he employed impropriety of a high degree? Hadn't he joined the war party without proper credentials! Hadn't he violated the strict code of the warrior society? But wasn't he as tenacious and determined as a wounded grizzly, one who would tough it out in battle or be struck down? The way he responded in the tight situation, thinking clearly and objectively, was another factor in his favor. Wasn't he an inspiration to the seasoned veterans? And didn't he make the first coup? Yes, the chief decided, Slow must be given the honor due him.

Though a few Sioux were wounded, none was so severely injured he could not remain on his mount. The Crows lost a score of men. Their riderless horses were captured and trophies of the chase collected—lances, shields, knives, and quivers with arrows. The Sioux party headed for camp, but decided to remain on the open prairie overnight and rest so the warriors at daybreak could charge into camp and announce the victory. Entering camp the following morning, the warriors formed a single column, circling the outer tepees time after time—singing, shouting, and performing their own individual exploits, which contributed to the victory.

No one was prouder of Slow than Jumping Bull, his father, who shed tears of admiration. Beat there no heart with a more enthusiastic glow than his! He placed the boy on the most beautiful horse he owned, and he had the best, then led it around, asking the people to view his brave son. "He has struck the enemy, my son has. He is brave!" Jumping Bull shouted. "I now give him the name *Ta-tané-ka I-yo-taé-ke*," in English Sitting Bull. And the name change had more than symbolic significance! To show his great appreciation of a deserving son, the father gave a horse to each of four poor men in camp.

Young Sitting Bull sat his horse like a seasoned veteran, legs tightly set against the pony's body. From the prized panther skin under him he displayed a rhythmic beauty that made horse and rider one. He welcomed the applause of his playmates who already respected him, the shy smiles of the girls, and his acceptance by the warriors. In his quiet way he enjoyed the attention. Now fourteen winters old, suddenly he was a warrior in the strictest tradition. With his new distinction, he was permitted to participate in the victory dance that evening. Being first to strike the enemy, young

Sitting Bull was the hero of the celebration. He danced with pride to the pounding of bison-hide drums, leaning forward, sideways, placing feet just right in the dance. He was aware of his mother's love, the respect of his two sisters, the applause of his relatives and friends, and the fruits of victory. But young Sitting Bull dreamed about greater achievements. His star had just begun to shine!

Now elevated to a warrior status, young Sitting Bull could participate in bison hunts; in fact, he already was considered quite a hunter. In bow and arrow contests he was always at or near the top. He took special care of his pony and trained it to come at his call. Just as his father taught him, he knew that success in hunts, like success in battle, was initiated primarily by riding the fastest and best trained horse. Then the rider could introduce the action.

It so happened that meat from twenty thousand bison was needed yearly to feed the large Sioux camp. Young Sitting Bull studied the bison and learned to know the animal well. He thought of the bison as one to whom he was related—not merely an animal with greater strength and keener sense of smell than any warrior. It was the bison meat and hide and horns the Sioux needed; still, no more animals were killed than were needed. The bison, in fact all animals of the wild, were young Sitting Bull's friends. Hadn't birds given him warning when a slinking enemy approached? Hadn't wolves pointed out bison by continually circling the herd, knowing that the Indians took the parts of the animals they needed and left the remainder for them? Yes, to slaughter these bovine friends indiscriminately would be disgraceful. Thus Sioux from infancy were taught never to kill more than was needed for food. On that note, as young Sitting Bull released an arrow at a bison he would whisper. "The Hunkpapa are hungry. I must kill you. Forgive me!"

Young Sitting Bull also understood the fate of aged and injured bison. As they were fair game for predators, he realized their future rests with the violent law of the land. Wolfpacks on a hunt echo music through the acoustics of the silent prairie. What a lovely symphony to the packs but a song *of death to aged bison*. Still, wolves, like other creatures of the wild, follow the law of the untamed, their only law—SURVIVAL OF THE FITTEST!

Studying bison every season of the year, he learned not to imitate man; instead he imitated the bison. He watched them patiently—learning their secrets. In spring he saw the calves running to and fro protected by their mothers; in summer the bulls, fat and strong from the nourishing prairie grass, lowering heads, pushing, straining, battling fiercely over cows. In the autumn he saw the vast herds migrating southward, eating as they went. In the winter there were the lean stubborn few that chose not to go south, pawing the snow for the dry grass beneath, leaving crimson marks from their bleeding noses on the white surface.

Most of all, young Sitting Bull respected the bison because it would never give up—it would never retreat regardless of obstacles or danger—it feared nothing. The boy studied these qualities of courage, strength, and determination and displayed them himself in later years.

With meat in camp in short supply, a bison hunt was scheduled. Early one morning a band of chosen warriors, young Sitting Bull one of them, rode off singing the bison song, each hunter on his fleetest mount. Near the herd the men hidden by a ridge paused for the order to charge. At best, this was a period of suffocating secrecy. *Akichita* (Indian police), armed with war clubs, watched the warriors so none would advance prior to the charge signal, knowing that any false move would stampede the herd.

But the wind shifted and the bulls, always alert, got wind of the Sioux hunters, as a bison's sense of smell is incredibly sensitive. Hunters now had their weapons ready—some with lances, others with bow and arrows. When the charge signal was given, over the ridge and down the valley the warriors sailed, straining their mounts to the limit, each warrior shouting the chilling hunting cry. And the hunt was on! Heels of moccasioned feet pounded the ribs of the ponies rapidly approaching the herd. Heavy bellowing by the bulls warned all animals to make haste. Mother bison positioned herself between hunters and calf, thus to shield her progeny from flying arrows.

Through heavy dust clouds the ponies charged. There was no view ahead. Warriors dropped reins over their pony's necks or held them by their teeth, grabbing arrows from their quivers as the trained animals galloped hard to arrive alongside fat cows running behind the bulls. Both hands of the warriors now operated their weapons. As soon as an arrow dropped one animal, the pony moved to another, being guided by the rider, who shifted his weight to the

Buffalo Chase, by George Catlin.

side he wanted his pony to move. Some arrows were driven entirely through bison cows and slid along the ground on the opposite side.

Hundreds of hooves drumming the earth rumbled an urgent crescendo that made the ground tremble. Lost in the billowing dust, hunters depended on their mounts, which, somehow, found their way. Arrow after arrow stung the bison. An occasional pony tripped in a prairie dog hole, fell, and threw the rider, who was trampled by the herd or gored by a dying animal. Neither the hot sun beating down nor the clouds of choking, blinding dust that filtered into eyes and throat halted the hunters. The pungent odor of the beasts, the thundering noise of hooves, the frightening bellow, the swish of flying arrows that fell the heavy bodies—all acted as a stimulant to the excited huntsmen.

Soon, too soon for young hunters, the leader signaled shooting to stop, as enough bison had been killed to feed the camp. Police enforced the order. The fixed rule of the Sioux, "Kill no more bison than needed," was obeyed.

One white man who knew bison well, Frederick Ruxton, wrote: "No animal requires as much killing as the bison." Although this statement may not be true even for North American animals, as the grizzly bear surely is harder to kill, still it is true enough.

When the hunt ended, bison were in varying stages of death, for unless shot through brain or spine, they run an almost unbelievable distance before dropping. Even when struck through the heart, they frequently keep running with the herd, though more and more slowly before falling—especially if they see the pursuing hunters after the wound has been made. If hunters are not seen, the animal will stop and stand in its tracks, bracing itself, feet farther and farther apart, to remain upright. Painful indeed is the sight of the dying struggle of the huge beast! As unyielding as a wounded grizzly, it resists lying down to the end, conscious that once it is down it can never rise again. A bull, shot through the lungs, blood streaming from nose and mouth, tongue hanging, eyes bloodshot and rolling, body swaying from side to side, lifts his huge head and helplessly bellows his conscious impotence. To the last moment, he plants his legs farther and farther apart, but with lost hope. Swaying from side to side like a sailing vessel rolling in a storm at sea, slowly turning his head, he looks for the enemy that put him in this condition. Gradually his failing limbs refuse to support him, and with a convulsive tremor the once powerful beast falls on its side and no longer has motion or life.

Before long, the older people appear at the hunting site, particularly the women who share the skinning and butchering. An awesome task, meat and hides, piled on horses, are brought to camp. When the hunters return home there is singing and drum beating at every quarter. Then there is joyous preparation for a bountiful feast a few days hence.

Hard work fills the next few days. Meat hangs from tall frames above reach of dogs and wolves. When sun- and wind-dried, it will be stored for winter use. Busy are women making pemmican—pounding bison meat and wild cherries with pits removed and adding suet. Horns, thrown aside, wait to be carved into ladles, spoons, and other utensils by old men. Sinew is saved for thread and bowstrings, bones for hide scrapers, hooves for glue to bind the sinew to arrowpoint and feathers to shaft, and the long hair from the animal's neck to be braided into belts and ropes. Bladder skins are bursting with marrow from bones. Hides for robes and tepees are stretched and pegged to the ground. Women kneel over them, pulling away the flesh and scraping the hides to eliminate excess weight. On a few hides, brains, and marrow are being rubbed to make them soft and pliable. All the camp, it seems, rejoices in the success of the hunt—a prodigal gift of nature!

Then stories are told, especially to the young. Sitting Bull's father tells his son how Sioux hunted bison before the horse. Though he knew not that Spaniards were first to bring the present-day horse to America, he did know how Sioux hunted the bison prior to that time—a story handed from one generation to another. Hunkpapa warriors disguised as wolves, he said, approached the herd. Each hidden under a wolf skin, the warriors slowly crawled with bow and arrows into the wind. Bulls, knowing that wolves always follow the herd to feed on the old and the injured, detected nothing wrong when the disguised hunters approached and let arrows fly. And this was how the Sioux hunted bison before the horse!

Indian families were close, with clear duties for men and women, Men set schedules, hunted, and fought—not only with trespassers, but with enemy tribes. Long before whites came, plains soil drank the blood of bitter combatants, and success in warfare more than anything else led a path to the political leadership of the tribe. Young Sitting Bull's duties made him a proud boy. He was overjoyed with his responsibilities and accomplished each task with eminent pride. He was always involved—learning, serving, watching. Young Sitting Bull became a superior marksman with the bow and arrow, winning many contests. His calm manner in tight situations increased his stature among seasoned warriors. He learned to read signs of nature—a bird nervously chattering, blades of grass matted down where animal or human enemy recently passed, a broken twig, and the excited call of a wild animal signifying something was amiss. Each of these signs telegraphed a message.

Young Sitting Bull became expert at obliterating his own moccasin prints and hoofmarks of his pony, brushing them lightly with grass or twig. He had so many ways to evaporate from an enemy. With a burning desire to learn, he began to flake his own arrow points and spear points after watching old craftsmen perform the task. He studied the strange pale-face people coming from the direction of the rising sun. He watched the military with disbelief, those men in blue who cross Sioux lands without asking permission. He knew them only as enemies. Still he viewed them as fighters of an inferior grade. Never did they circle the enemy on their mounts like the Sioux. "They dismount to fight and become easy targets," he confided to no one in particular. "When a soldier is killed, nobody cares. When a Sioux is hit, we feel bad, pull him up on a pony, and carry him from the field of battle."

At camp one day, Sioux scouts detected a column of soldiers off in the distance. A dozen scouts rode ahead of the main body of warriors in an attempt to learn the soliders' intentions. When they were within gun range, shots rang out and two warriors fell. This confrontation so angered the Sioux that an avalanche of warriors attacked the bluecoats and more shots were fired.

Noticing that the guns were single-shot, the warriors charged the soldiers with their bows, arrows, and spears before muskets could be reloaded, as a bow-and-arrow weapon is a repeater as long as arrows are in the quiver.

Hand-to-hand fighting was violent. A soldier, swinging his gun explosively, knocked a Sioux from his horse, hitting the warrior over the head with the gun stock. Young Sitting Bull, hanging on the opposite side of his mount to be as small a target as possible, raced his pony to assist his comrade. But the soldier fired a large-caliber pistol, hitting Sitting Bull in the hip. The bullet passed through his body, coming out the back. Despite the wound, Sitting Bull dispatched the soldier and sat his mount until the battle ended. At camp the wound was treated, and in a few days the young warrior was up and around.

During 1856, by white man's calendar, and Winter-When-the-War-Bonnet-Was-Torn, by the Sioux calendar, wise men of the tribe realized that more horses were needed. Winters in Sioux country were so severe that only a few colts survived. The best horses were in Mexico and Texas, and the Comanche tribe, whose territory bordered on these lands, stole their horses and traded them to tribes farther north. Hunkpapa hierarchy decided that stealing rather than trading for them was the best deal, with excitement and glory thrown in for good measure.

The Hunkpapa at this time were encamped on a Yellowstone River tributary between Box Elder and Powder River. Scouts reported that the Crows, the Sioux's perpetual enemy to the south, had recently acquired a large herd from the Comanches and thought this an appropriate time to share these animals. Ridding the Crows of horses would materially weaken their striking force. So a hundred Hunkpapa volunteered for the grueling expedition; about half were young men without mounts, walking the entire distance carrying lariats and saddle pads. For these, a trip of this magnitude could contribute handsomely toward their warrior dreams.

Sitting Bull recently had been promoted to sash bearer of the prestigious Strong Hearts Warrior Society. Mounted, he proudly carried a shield and a new weapon, a smoothbore muzzle-loader gun. Being chosen by the chief for the expedition was a signal honor in itself.

Days of travel ensued, following a carefully selected route to the huge Crow camp. Finally, on a day clear as an eagle's eye, the camp and horse herd were spotted in the far distance. As the Sioux remained hidden behind a ridge, plans were formulated for the nighttime escapade. During darkness, a sizable herd was quietly assembled and driven away, with young men now mounted. Pushing their quarry hard ahead of them, the Hunkpapas headed for home—some warriors riding point on the herd, some the flanks, while the main body drove from the rear. This latter group would feel the Crow pursuers' sting first.

About midday, disenchanted Crow warriors shouting their battle cry charged over a hilltop just passed. Down the hill, like water pouring down an abyss, they floated. Closing in on their stolen prize, the Hunkpapa formed an outer battle line. Within a quarter-mile of this line, the Crow attackers stopped short. Three Crow leaders, one the chief, challenged three Sioux to hand-to-hand combat. The Hunkpapa accommodated them. Sitting Bull, one of the three, leaped from horse. Deadly serious, he yelled to the Crow Chief, "I'll fight you! I'm Sitting Bull!"

Wearing a chief's insignia on his red leather vest trimmed with ermine tails, the muscular chief, with powerful arms shining like polished granite, waved a gun high over his head, finger on the trigger, A powder horn hung from his shoulder. Both warriors had steel knives in their belts. The chief knew Sitting Bull would fight to the death inasmuch as he was singing the Strong Heart death song:

>Comrades, whoever runs way
>>He is a woman, so they say;
>Through fight and many trials,
>>My life is meant to be short.

Sitting Bull ran toward the chief, who leaped from his mount and stood rigid for a moment. The Crow leader actually had challenged a Hunkpapa warrior to a "hand-to-hand combat," although Sitting Bull noticed the chief was readying his gun to take aim. Sitting Bull also had a charge in his weapon, and if the Crow chief misunderstood or reneged on his mode of combat, Sitting Bull would make this charge count. He would honor their agreement and not fire first, however. Now the two antagonists were almost together. Raising his gun, the chief fired. Sitting Bull, watching his every move, dropped to one knee, holding the shield ahead of him with one hand and discharging his weapon with the other. At that moment he felt the armor spring back as the ball pierced it near the edge where a shield is thin and felt a burning pain in his left foot. But the Crow chief fell to his knees, shot through the body. Despite the painful wound, Sitting Bull sprang forward and lunged his knife into the Crow chief's heart.

Seeing their leader struck down, the Crows, including the other two challengers, let no prairie grass grow under their ponies' feet, leaving the Hunkpapa with the horse herd. In a daring display of determination, Sitting Bull struggled to his horse, refused any assistance in mounting, and rode away with the others. In camp it was learned that the musket ball had struck the left foot between the toes, plowed through the foot, and exited at the heel, leaving Sitting Bull forever with a pronounced limp. But Hunkpapa warriors who viewed the battle remembered his gallant bravery, and the deed would surface later in Sitting Bull's future.

Time moved on. Enemies changed. Sioux now were less concerned about their old enemy, the Crows, realizing that while the tribes were fighting over inches, the militiary was taking miles. In turn the Crows worried less about the Sioux. After all, weren't they

Fort McKenzie, with the Combat 28 Aug 1833, by Charles Bodmer. The Boston Athenaeum.

all Indians? So they dramatically refocused their sights on the white upstarts new to the land—those wearing blue uniforms.

Just ended was the War between the States. The white nation was almost bankrupt. "Roads to the western gold fields must be opened," officials in Washington demanded. "This precious metal is our only chance to liquidate the accruing interest of the national debt." Quite remarkably, Congress in those days actually attempted to pay off the national debt!

White people, like an unwanted shadow, poured into Indian lands, and Sitting Bull's heart grew sad. "Why do they come and drive away our bison? Indians must have bison to live. We will defend our bison, our land, and our people."

White soldiers came. More soldiers, in a maneuver the military assumed would terrorize the wicked into righteousness. The Sioux could not understand. Where did all the white people come from? The Sioux did not know the world had so many white people. Where had they been?

Chief Crazy Horse of the Oglala Sioux remarked with concern, "Why have the white people come, those who destroy the earth and its life, who take the beautiful world away from the Indians and make it into a senseless place where the true things of the Spirit are forgotten because they put gold and the things it will buy first? What can we do to stop them?"

Trouble at first was avoided by the Sioux merely by ignoring the military. Oftentimes army guns shot at the Sioux warriors and they fell, but then so did soldiers. Sitting Bull personally participated in several skirmishes. His war songs were many, and his favorite contained these words:

> No chance for me to live;
> Mother, you might as well mourn!

The song shows the deep love Sitting Bull carried for his mother. In his youth before he left camp to engage an enemy, his mother oftentimes pleaded for him to remain behind the rest occasionally. "Don't always be first," she cautioned. "The first always die."

Years passed. Sitting Bull grew to manhood. Thirty-five winters old, married, and with three children, he had won every honor open to a Sioux warrior except death. Presently leader of war parties, he knew what it was to suffer pain, and although he knew it not, more would come. Even now he was lamed for life from a Crow chief's bullet that had passed completely through his foot, breaking bones and severing tendons.

And white soldiers kept coming; they were seemingly endless. Sioux could not understand why. On came one column, comprising about one thousand men, which extended into the distance. Sioux patience now was thin—warriors approached the column with extreme caution. Sitting Bull motioned the military leader for a talk, to ask why so many soldiers were moving back and forth over their best bison hunting grounds. Without warning, fitful flashes from soldiers' guns telegraphed their agonizing message. Several Indians fell, although Sitting Bull was not hit. When the order "Charge the soldiers!" was shouted, warriors with guns shot back. But most Sioux still had the bow and the lance that called for infighting. Yet Sioux blood called for enemy blood—death inflamed their desire for revenge.

Cavalry mounts traveled far that day, so far that the animals appeared downright fatigued. Detecting this weakness, the Sioux orchestrated an attack in force—one group charging in, then another. The cavalry headed for higher ground to continue the battle, but the fresh Indian ponies cut ahead of the overworked cavalry mounts. With the bugle sounding retreat, the soldiers forced a breakthrough. Soldiers and Indians fell—many never to rise again. Firing arrows and musket balls into the retreating bluecoats, the battle became a rout. Sitting Bull on his sorrel pony fought with valor and determination, inspiring Sioux warriors at every turn. His single-shot muzzle-loader was empty, and he had spent his lance on a soldier earlier. With gun raised over his head, he gave the signal to stop the attack.

Accounts of the battle by the commanding officer at the fort were uncomplimentary to the military. He said the troops had been driven from Sioux lands by a smaller force of Indians and that the soldiers "disgraced the government," in a statement undoubtedly true, but quite unique for the military.

Surprisingly, the Sioux at this very time thought the prestige of their fighting force was declining inasmuch as white man's military force traveled virtually unrestricted through Sioux lands. Thinking men of the tribes had a growing feeling of uncertainity. To them it was painfully clear the Sioux nation had fallen asleep in the eye of the storm and they saw an urgent need to rouse it from dormancy. They felt the nation should reorganize to gain greater strength—strength that no single tribe within could possess alone. Tribal chiefs had failed to live up to expectations, i.e., all except Four Horns, an aging leader with seemingly endless energy and phenomenal foresight.

A spectrum of options was considered, but Four Horns thought the Sioux nation should have a single leader, one chief who would unify all the Sioux people while at the same time restoring the great honor of chieftancy—a veritable walk from the past into the future. So Four Horns led the way. Although he had two sons eligible for the position, he passed them by. But his nephew, Sitting, Bull, head of the Midnight Strong Hearts, a warrior society of distinction, was something else. He had the necessary qualifications! Chief Four Horns visualized "strong medicine" leadership possibilities for Sitting Bull—the warrior who led almost every successful charge against Sioux enemies. Here was a warrior with many coups, one who was twice wounded in the heat of battle—once so severely he was lamed for life. Here was a peacemaker among his people—one who could restore order and prestige to the Sioux nation and one whom old and young would respect. Here was a generous man, always capturing horses from the enemy and giving them to the poor of the tribe. Here was a bison hunter of excellence, and here was a fiery, convincing orator. Still, he could tell humorous stories with the best. Furthermore, Sitting Bull held the gift of prophecy—foretelling the results of a coming battle with surprising accuracy. He was a deeply religious man, and his prayers were answered regularly. And here was a man who would maintain Sioux customs and laws and would protect their vast bison hunting grounds from all enemies. Last but not least, Four Horns knew that Sitting Bull had the full support of the prestigious Midnight Strong Hearts warrior society without whose approval no chief could reign. And hadn't this society under Sitting Bull's leadership grown to over two hundred members?

Recommending a close relative for a high position was virtually sacrilegious. Still, Chief Four Horns stood his ground, endorsing his nephew Sitting Bull. At a special meeting the Midnight Strong Hearts verbally promoted their popular leader. Warriors at the meeting reiterated some of Sitting Bull's achievements—the battle in which he killed the Crow chief, the time he saved a fellow warrior from certain death during a savage battle, the day he was shot and continued the fight until victory was achieved, and the time he was shot through the foot and crippled for life. Yes, they related, Sitting Bull's honors were legion.

But Four Horns needed further support—that of the counselors, those grizzled old men with influence who made the Sioux nation the power it was. These men of authority, whose memories retrogressed into places the young had never been, would judge Sitting Bull not only as a leader to win enemy battles, but as a civil leader who would unite the tribe and keep it powerful. When Four Horns spoke, the great warriors of the past generation sat rigid, fixed. Their eyes were riveted on Four Horns. Serious was the tone of the meeting, but then, one after the other rose and spoke. Each praised Sitting Bull—his keen mind, his ability to organize, his concern for all the people of the tribe. It was Sitting Bull all the way!

Yet to make this radical change, to create a single high command, all tribes of the loose Sioux nation must be counseled. Four Horns traveled afar and presented the proposal to these chiefs, emphasizing the need to organize the Sioux nation into a fighting force capable of resisting their new, powerful enemy—the military. Agreement was reached. Sitting Bull it would be.

So their designated new leader was called to a meeting where at a pretentious ceremony he was appointed head chief. And it was Four Horns who orated, "Because of your bravery and your position as the greatest warrior of all our people, we have elected you, Sitting Bull, the head chief of our Sioux nation. It is your duty to see that we are fed. When you say, 'Fight,' we will fight; when you say, 'Let us make peace,' we will make peace."

Then Crazy Horse of the Oglala Sioux, many winters younger than Sitting Bull, also a warrior of renown, was appointed second in command. He, too, had an enviable record on the field of battle, unequaled by anyone except Sitting Bull. He too was generous to the poor, having given away almost all possessions save two horses and his fighting weapons. Sitting Bull respected the credulity of

Crazy Horse so highly that the two met together prior to every major tribal decision.

Near the end of the ceremony, Sitting Bull was presented with a bow and ten arrows, as well as a new musket recently taken from the military. He was told to follow the spirit of the eagle, chief of all birds—one that flies above every known thing. Placed on his head was a war bonnet, superbly decorated with beads, ermine pendants, and eagle plumes. It carried a train of eagle tail feathers reaching to the ground. He was told that each feather was symbolic of a coup or other brave deed performed by the warriors who contributed to the headdress. Thus Sitting Bull was crowned publicly.

A beautiful horse, all white, was brought forth and Sitting Bull was lifted gently into the saddle. The horse was slowly led around the ceremonical circle with members of the warrior societies following; Midnight Strong Hearts, Crow Owners, Night Riders, Badgers, Fox Soldiers, and Mandan—all dressed in new buckskin and mountain sheep garments decorated with porcupine quills and colored beads. Faces painted for war, shields uncovered, bows strung, and arrows firmly held, the warriors chanted Sioux war songs. Leading the procession was the bravest warrior of the Sioux nation, a man now lame, but competent, kind, generous, and determined—one who had risen from humble beginnings to the highest rank, head chief!

VII

Sitting Bull Wins the Big One

Peace on the Great Plains turned out to be as fragile as an Indian clay pot. The Sioux nation, now a powerful confederacy of Blackfoot Sioux, Brule, Hunkpapa, Minniconjou, Oglala, Sans Arc, and Two Kettles, tenaciously united for self-defense. Superior horseman expertise came naturally from perpetual war with neighboring tribes: Assiniboine, Blackfeet, Cheyenne, Cree, Crow, Chippewa, Comanche, Flathead, Gros Ventres, Kiowa, Ree, and Shoshone. Yet these Sioux somehow had energy to raid those less aggressive tribes such as the Iowa, Kansas, Mandan, Missouri, Nez Perce, Omaha, Osage, Oto, Ponca, and Ute. At this very time, head chief Sitting Bull made his position clear. He warned whites that Sioux would tolerate no indiscriminate bison killing, which friendly as well as enemy Indian tribes honored. "Without bison," he orated time and again, "my people cannot live!" Yet he at first held no deep animosity toward white people and would not allow his warriors to eradicate settlements scattered over Sioux bison hunting grounds.

Combative as a mountain ram in his native Black Hills, Sitting Bull made these poignant demands: keep the military off Sioux land; take down the forts erected without Sioux permission; close the military roads; keep steamboats away from Sioux waters. "No good we keep dancing around the fire. White man must keep his word, follow treaties his chief in Washington made with us. Only then we have peace. If word not kept, Sioux will fight!"

Sitting Bull's peaceful intention was openly displayed when he permitted the Northern Pacific Railroad survey crew to travel unmolested for some hundred miles over Sioux land—until the military was made its guardian. An agreement between the tribe and government existed, permitting the Northern Pacific to build a railroad along the north bank of the Yellowstone River, but only the north bank, as bison herds regularly followed the south bank. Disregarding this agreement and backed by the military, the crew began surveying a right-of-way along the controversial south bank. Although Sitting Bull at the time was encamped along Powder River miles away, he had scouts watching both crew and military. They reported, distressfully, that the crew was setting stakes for a railroad right-of-way along the south bank of the river. Sharply castigating the whites, whom he said do not keep their word, Sitting Bull met with a group of selected warriors and orated, "They have insulted Sioux intelligence! Let us talk to them" and he left immediately with a small party to discuss the matter with the military officer in charge.

Dressed in war regalia and carrying weapons, Sitting Bull rode the darkness through. Whether on peace or war missions, when meeting strangers for council a Sioux Chief dressed in this fashion. Astride his fleet bay pony, the head chief carried a gun. In the quiver hanging over his shoulder was a bow and stone-tipped arrows. He rode ahead of the twenty-two warriors personally selected for the trip and chose this small group so the military would understand his mission was peaceful. He merely wished to talk to the commander and persuade him to remove the survey crew from the south bank of the Yellowstone and the military force from Sioux land.

At daybreak the Sioux party reached the huge military camp. Always alert, Sitting Bull approached cautiously, arm raised, signaling a friendly greeting. When within gun range, a shot was fired at him. The bullet narrowly missed. More shots came. Returning to his warrior band a short distance behind, painfully he shouted this diatribe: "Did not the soldiers shoot first? Does not the military choose to fight rather than have council? If it wants to fight, let us fight. Come!" His men followed.

Crazy Horse, second in command of the Sioux nation and considered one of the best fighters on the plains, was a member of the party. Face painted with white spots as usual, his hair hung loose. Dressed in white buckskin shirt and "leggins," though privileged to wear an assortment of feathers, he wore none. He carried a lance and shield—nothing more. Slim, medium height, with a light complexion and a serious expression, he rode gracefully with body erect, looking like the great warrior he really was.

Charging the military camp, the Indians unloaded a volley, then galloped their steeds out of gun range. Crazy Horse led charge after charge. Miraculously, he was not hit. Sitting Bull, seeing his second in command displaying such phenomenal bravery, no longer could endure the challenge. He was forced to demonstrate he was the streaking nova that eclipsed all other stars of the Sioux complex. Dismounting within rifle range of the soliders, coolly laying down his gun and quiver, then taking out his pipe and tobacco pouch, he sat down and smoked. He was openly showing the military that he was ready to smoke with the commander, but also was reminding Crazy Horse and his Sioux warriors the quality of bravery their head chief possessed. Such raw courage the soldiers did not know existed in anyone, let alone Indians. Shocked by this display of fearlessness, the soldiers held their fire for a moment. But Sitting Bull hadn't finished. Turning his head toward his warriors, he shouted so the interpreters for the military could hear, "Those who wish to smoke come here!" And several warriors joined him, but not the military commander.

Fire again was spitting from soldier's guns. Dust exploded where musket balls struck the ground around the head chief and his men. A warrior, hit, fell off his pony and was taken from gunshot range. Smoking the peace pipe, Sitting Bull sat calmly. With bullets spattering around him, he portrayed an image of indestructability. Such boldness, such cool recklessness under fire, beat anything the military had ever seen. Why Sitting Bull was not hit cannot be explained. This exhibition of courage, though magnificent, was not a coup—he touched no enemy—but it was bravery at its best. It taught Sioux warriors the true meaning of the word.

Indians by skillful use of shields persistently charged the military encampment—shooting arrows and bullets at the soldiers, then racing their ponies back to their own line. Crazy Horse, leading, had his horse shot from under him. Running zigzag out of enemy musket range, he caught the horse of a warrior who was killed and continued leading the charges. Outnumbered at least ten to one, nonetheless, the Sioux gave a good account of themselves.

Now sitting on his pony, the chief was satisfied that the commander would not talk. "Stop!" he called to his warriors. "That is enough. He will not talk." It was high noon. Taking the dead and injured with them, Sitting Bull's party returned to camp at Powder

River. Though it was a savage encounter, it was nothing compared to bloody forthcoming battles, inasmuch as the two forces were wholly irreconcilable. The military now was convinced the Sioux nation was serious about defending itself—and its bison. Yet Sitting Bull did not consider his tribe at war with whites. But the military—that was a different breed of prairie dogs!

News of the encounter that provoked a tornado of uncertainties spread rapidly by pony legs and smoke signals. All Indian camps were placed on alert. Despite the growing tension, two winters quietly passed. But then the government decided to establish a military post in the Black Hills in addition to Fort Abraham Lincoln on the Missouri River near today's Mandan, North Dakota. To the Sioux this was interpreted as "changing the rules in the middle of the game." It seems the only thing on which they could agree was that there was nothing on which they could agree. The irresistible military force met an unyielding object. Sitting Bull now realized that rough days were ahead.

Old Jim Bridger, a shrewd mountain-man trapper if there ever was one, who had the confidence of both Indians and whites, cautioned the government, "The Sioux will never permit a fort in the center of their bison hunting grounds. And to connect it by military roads to other forts? This is rubbing salt into the wound!" To the Sioux, much had been conceded to the government when the tribe agreed to let the iron horse travel the north bank of the Yellowstone. But the south bank? Never!

Displaying its power, the military sent Gen.[1] George Armstrong Custer westward from Fort Abraham Lincoln. His orders? Raid Sioux villages and destroy Indian ponies. Establishing Fort Abraham Lincoln itself violated a treaty the government had with the Sioux.

Custer's march through the Black Hills went unchallenged. Upon his return to the fort, never failing to publicize and promote, Custer gave the world through the press a scintillating account of the country. "Gold is everywhere," he was quoted as saying. And an "invasion by osmosis" began. Headlines appeared in newspapers over the nation. And the rush was on! Miners drawn like a magnet dashed in to make a fortune. Traders followed on their heels. And

---

[1] A Civil War brevet commission. Militarily Lieutenant Colonel Custer.

A dog's life! Breaking camp before the horse.

the military? It stood by, making no attempt to quell the invasion, although at this late moment it may not have succeeded had it tried. Sitting Bull, alert to what was going on, again met with his chiefs inasmuch as the tribe now faced excruciating decisions. "Is this not trespass?" he bitingly asked. "Did Sioux not have these lands for many moons—long before white man came?" Accordingly, defense strategems were formulated!

For three decades the Indian Bureau had worked peacefully with the Sioux, and its accomplishments were notable. Now Custer's march reversed engines, canceling all the good work the bureau had achieved over the years. Sitting Bull was not taking the trespass of the Black Hills lightly, as the Black Hills, effervescing the discriminating flavor of the Rockies were the most precious part of the Sioux domain. Here was a land so dear the Indians called it sacred. Here was where the Sioux for generations climbed the peaks to pray. Here was a place teeming with wildlife and streams overflowing with fish. And nowhere in the Sioux domain were there lovelier pastoral valleys and forested peaks. Imposing, most assuredly, but lacking the harsh ruggedness of the great Rockies farther west. So the Black Hills had a feeling all their own, a friendly feeling of home to the Sioux, offering them rest and comfort. Sitting Bull now cautioned his people, "Do you not see that white chief in Washington speaks with forked tongue?[1] White man cannot be trusted!"

---

[1] Referring to the forked tongue of the prairie rattlesnake, whose bite was painful and occasionally deadly.

Seeing the Black Hills as the pathway to prosperity, white people raced to settle them. Miners, traders, and settlers took possession. Instead of moving the people out to comply with the treaty, the army was assigned to protect them. Then the government wanted to buy the Black Hills. Approached, Sitting Bull made his position crystal clear: "We have no land to sell. Black Hills belong to the Great Spirit. They are a treasure beyond price and are ours only to protect, which we have done for many moons." He then delivered this impassioned plea, "If soldiers try to take them, we will fight!"

And the settlement of the Black Hills became permanent. Wildlife of the hills gave way to the wealthy society of successful miners and businessmen. The village Deadwood appeared. Still the Sioux did not attack the settlement, claiming that unarmed miners and settlers were not their enemy. But then things suddenly changed. Miners took up arms. So did the settlers! Skirmishes between them and Indians became frequent. Young warriors, itching for revenge, wanted to drive all whites from the Black Hills or kill them. And it almost happened! Only Sitting Bull's persuasive oratory prevented a massacre. Day by day the military might of the hills increased. The army had taken the dream out of the Indian dreamworld.

During an autumn bison hunt, a Sioux party found a starving white man aimlessly wandering over the prairie. His footsteps screamed in silence. He was eating grasshoppers and the bark and leaves of plants he found. His faded blue uniform torn to shreds, much too large for his starved frame, was mute evidence that the man, once muscular, was an army deserter. A young warrior, detecting the blue military coat, set an arrow against his bowstring, readying for the kill. Sitting Bull quickly pulled the arrow down, saying, "Do not kill him. See? He has no gun and no horse. He is leaving our country." The Indians gave him water and food. Sitting Bull only asked that he leave Sioux land.

The repeating rifle had now been invented, and Sitting Bull owned the first in the Sioux camp. The syncopated meter and tune of this repeater played an inspiring refrain to his warriors in many battles. The weapon was a gift from Bad Soup, a daring bowman who had taken it from a military officer whose heart was pierced by Bad Soup's arrow. But in the Sioux camp was an even bigger requisite: horses—needed so that young warriors would have mounts. And replacements for horses lost in battle were vital. The best animals, Sitting Bull concluded, were those stolen from Mexicans by an enemy tribe bordering their territory on the south. So the Sioux went on a raiding party. They went to steal horses—horses taken from the Mexicans.

The trip required several days of travel. And what happened en route? Nothing except trouble finding water for their horses after they left known country. Their own drinking water was carried in special containers. And how did Sitting Bull's legion find water for their mounts? The strategy was simple. Knowing that a thirsty horse can smell water for an incredible distance, Sitting Bull had his warriors string their horses across a wide expanse as they advanced. When a horse began to race in a direct line, disregarding efforts of the mounted warrior to change his course, water soon was located.

Reaching a low ridge overlooking the enemy camp, the raiding party saw a herd of horses tethered near the tepees. These apparently had been recently stolen from the Mexicans and were not yet trusted to run with the grazing herd. Plans, meticulously prepared, called for approaching the camp late at night when occupants were asleep, selecting the best animals, then hurrying home. Sitting Bull was an old master at stealing horses. Satisfied that he could accomplish the feat without detection, he was not so sure about others in the party. A warrior might misjudge somewhere and awaken the camp. Then the raiding party would fight to force its way out, leaving a warrior or two behind. Sitting Bull knew every trick of horse thievery, yet as usual, he asked for guidance from above. Raising his arms in the black of night, palms skyward, he prayed for help.

Tethering their own horses on the flat prairieland a few miles away, the Sioux stealthily approached the sleeping camp, located around a large spring. The head chief, now lame, walked with a pronounced limp. Still he could sneak and crawl with the best. He had planned every detail in his usual unerring fashion. Knowing that ill-tempered dogs would be all over the place, they were included. Raiding the camp was high drama.

Approaching in darkness, crawling, listening, moving with body flat on the ground, the Sioux finally neared the outer ring of tepees. Suddenly, excitedly, a dog barked. Other joined in. The fresh bison meat, carried for the purpose, was thrown to them.

Sitting Bull knew that dogs could not bark and eat at the same time. And Indian dogs were always hungry. This same trick, used by the head chief at other raids, was a sure-fire success.

Nearing the horses, Sitting Bull heard the bell of the lead animal. Methodically crawling in the animal's direction, silhouetted against the paler sky he saw the most beautiful black horse he had ever seen. Rising slowly, patting the animal, he cut the bell-strap. Slipping a lariat around the horse's neck, he gently stroked him. Then he cut the rawhide rope tied around its nose and neck. Using this rope, a bridle was improvised by looping the rawhide about the animal's nose and jaw. As expected, the horse was gentle—and a black beauty. Sliding onto its bare back, Sitting Bull rode quietly from the enemy camp.

Others of the Sioux party were equally busy selecting the best animals they could find. They too made crude bridles from lariats, performing the tasks quietly and swiftly. Meeting at a prearranged location, each warrior had a fine horse. Recoving their own ponies, leading them, they hurried away in darkness, knowing that by sunup enemy warriors with their eyes blazing fire would be in hot pursuit.

Catching crafty Sitting Bull was no Sunday picnic. He knew more tricks to confuse pursuers than a prairieland fox. When the soft morning rays of light broke through grassland haze, the Sioux were a good twenty miles from the Indian camp. Coming to the stream Sitting Bull remembered when traveling south, the ponies were directed into its water. Tracks down the stream bank were hurriedly obliterated and the forced march continued. Proceeding upstream until an appropriate exit was reached, again the pony tracks were eliminated by brushing them lightly with tree branches. This strategy Sitting Bull knew would delay the pursuers if not lose them completely. After a few more miles the warriors again changed mounts—riding one and leading the other. This change of mounts was almost like white man's Pony Express. Horses were pushed to the limit. Whenever the one being ridden was tiring, a change was made to the other. The forced march brought the raiding party home in a mere few days, each Hunkpapa leading a fine horse. And this raid, like others before it, supplied the Sioux with most of their fleet ponies!

And what was happening on the Black Hills frontiers? As the miners, traders, and settlers increased, their influence and demands

A squaw's work—erecting the bisonhide tepee.

on Washington increased proportionately. When the army was ordered to defend whites indiscriminately, Sitting Bull lost all hope for a peaceful settlement. The breaking point had been reached. Hatred grew! Skirmishes were common. When an eastern market for bison robes developed, hordes of professional white hunters invaded the southern plains, using high-powered Sharps rifles. The slaughter began. Bison were killed by the thousands, hides taken, and the corpses left on the plains. Then railroads came, pushing their right-of-ways westward. A high-protein food was needed for those laying the tracks. What food was used? Bison meat! And so the slaughter of bison on the southern plains accelerated.

  The government now knew how to suppress western tribes without direct confrontation. How? By eliminating the bison! If these were destroyed, Indians of the plains also would be destroyed, as bison meant everything to them. By 1874 white hunters, orchestrating attacks on bison mainly for hides, brought ruin to the Plains

Indian economy. Having killed millions of the bovines on the southern plains, they moved northward to continue the slaughter. Bloodiest of all Indians battles at this stage came when the lordly Cheyenne to the south, powerful in their own right and with superb horses "borrowed for keeps" from their Mexican neighbors, clashed with these testy Sioux. But pressure by hunters, settlers, and the military accelerated, forcing these vigilant Cheyenne to join hands with their principal enemy, the Sioux, whose domain lay farther north, thus to save themselves from what they considered virtual extinction. Tribes realized their days might be numbered. So enraged they became that old enemies united and formed a confederacy of resistance. Sioux and Cheyenne especially, strong and cavalier, would not jump to the crack of the military whip. Aware of government strategy, they knew that without bison there would be no food in their tepees. To avoid a bloody conflict they moved northwest, where bison still roamed freedly inasmuch as white hunters had not yet arrived at this location. Here the Sioux, Cheyenne, and others pledged resistance to the last breath! Bison were not the only targets on the plains. It was reported that some of the military companies at the time shot at every Indian seen, attempting to wipe out both friendly and unfriendly tribes. "The Indian must be put in his place," was a popular saying. "His place" apparently meant the Happy Hunting Ground.

    Sitting Bull, proud, capable, determined, would not yield to the military, the recognized symbol of U.S. authority. Around a campfire he was quiet and gentle, but when the military came his way he became a tiger. Hypersensitive to the rights of the Sioux, he agonized, "If they want war we will oblige. There is a limit to what even a friendly songbird will bear." Mocassioned runners and pony riders fanned out in all directions. To every tribe they went, in fact, to all Sioux, Cheyenne, Arapaho, and lesser tribes on the Great Plains. Smoke signals also telegraphed the chilling message. News spread like a wind-driven prairie fire. Young warriors especially, energetic, loyal, and confident, willingly accepted the challenge. Skirmishes with the military at several points were won, giving warriors added encouragement. Many soldiers had been killed. But as soon as one company was put out of commission, another, sometimes two, took its place. Where were all the soldiers coming from, the Indians wondered. Surely there is a limit! A fog of uncertainity clouded the question. What Sitting Bull didn't know and had no way to find out, was that the white population of the nation disproportionately outnumbered his Sioux by more than five hundred to one.

But Sitting Bull was no one to panic. Always the master strategist, he took extraordinary precautions at every turn. He sent scouts far and wide, watching the movement of soldiers. "Soldiers seem to be everywhere," he reported at a council meeting. Like a tropical storm, he rained epithets on the military. Messages were flashed from ridge to ridge, and the Sioux camps moved northwestward following the decreasng bison herds.

Encamped along a spring-fed creek between the Rosebud and Little Big Horn rivers Sitting Bull on June 16, 1876, was brought "bad news" by a scout. The valley along the Rosebud was alive with bluecoats. By now the head chief was organized for defense, having the Cheyennes and other tribes with him. About half his warriors had guns, taken as military men fell—the remainder of the Indians had bows, arrows, and lances. But the military, by now, had "muddied the waters!"

Hurriedly assembling a determined party of Indians, faces and bodies painted, dressed in war regalia, the mounted warriors paraded single file around camp. Through darkness they traveled—arriving at the military encampment at daybreak. General Crook, called "Three Stars," had about one thousand white soldiers and two hundred Indians, the latter being Crows, Rees, and Shoshoni, longtime enemies of the Sioux. Three Stars had been sent to weaken the Sioux conscience and destroy the Indians' will to fight back. All his men had guns. Sitting Bull, carrying his repeating rifle on this trip, wore two eagles feathers in this hair. He was older now and the task of organizing the party and the all-night ride had tired him. He chose to direct operations rather than participate physically in the melee.

As soon as the Indians came within rifle range of the military camp, shots at them were fired and these were answered with a blizzard of arrows. This reception triggered a Sioux charge that hit the military like a swarm of enraged hornets. Sitting Bull, atop his horse nearby, coolly directed operations. In low, mellow voice he called, "Steady, warriors. Aim accurately. Make every shot count!" Crazy Horse, much younger and a superior horseman, led the charges.

Body hidden on the side of his pony, only the top of his head visible to the soldiers, he and the others discharged their weapons, then raced out of range. The battle lasted all day, with heavy casualties suffered by the military and the Sioux. At evening General Crook moved off, heading for the fort from where he came. He had had enough. Sitting Bull had put Crook's army out of commission.

Despite heavy losses, success to the Sioux and Cheyenne was sweet. Riding home, carrying dead and injured, ammunition and arrows spent, they rejoiced in "Victory." "Didn't the soldiers retreat to the safety of the fort? Didn't we drive them from our bison hunting grounds?" they shouted.

The rapidly growing Indian camp now moved often. Hundreds of acres of prairie grass were required to feed the pony herd. No less, the people needed food—bison. But where horses grazed and lodges dotted the prairie grass, there were no bison; the shaggy bovines simply moved away. Hunting the beasts miles yonder, then bringing the meat and hides to camp was a formidable task. Nevertheless, those in camp were fed well. Sitting Bull remembered that the Sioux a year earlier had hunted along the Little Big Horn River at a tributary called Greasy Grass. There the rich forage made

Custer's Last Fight.

Courtesy of Anheuser Busch, Inc.

meat of bison sweet and juicy and Sioux ponies became muscular and strong. He decided to move camp to this distant location.

Moving day was June 22, 1876. A seemingly endless wave of humanity, consolidated for protection, moved northward over the flat prairie. Indians afoot and mounted, loose horses running to nowhere, pack animals led, and dogs pulling miniature travois straggled along, an uneven column over the prairie ocean. Scouts ahead, behind, and on the flanks studied the horizon for soldiers. From a distance this motley caravan resembled tumbleweeds rolling over the landscape. Families unhesitatingly surrendered control of their fate to Sitting Bull. Each traveled as a unit, except for the warrior guards assigned to specific defensive positions. So long was the column the Cheyennes in the lead, five hundred lodges strong, had pitched their tepees and finished the evening meal before Sitting Bull's own Hunkpapa Sioux, whom he had travel last, reached its campsite. Following the Cheyenne were the Oglala Sioux with four hundred lodges, and next came the Sans Arc, the Minniconjou, and the Brules, with another four hundred tepees. The Hunkpapa, including a few unidentified tribes, comprised five hundred lodges.

Farthest north on the Little Big Horn River west bank sat the circle of Cheyenne lodges. As was the case with other tribes, each family set its tepee in its designated space. South, about a mile upriver, was the Sans Arc Sioux circle. Then came the Minniconjou and Brules. West, along Medicine Creek, was the Oglala circle of lodges. The Hunkpapa camp, also housing the Blackfeet Sioux, Two Kettles, and Santees, was stationed along the Little Big Horn about a mile upriver from the Minniconjou and Brules. Thus a city of 1,800 lodges, housing no fewer than two thousand bison hunters and fierce fighters extraordinary, decorated for three miles the prairieland bordering the west bank of the Little Big Horn.

And this huge assemblage of lodges had police protection. Sitting Bull saw to that. Nights, mounted warriors circled each group, singing and calling out assurances that all was well. Added security was established by scouts stationed at more distant points. Yet the old and the wise were uneasy, sensing an impending battle that might change their entire lives.

For two days the tribes readied themselves for a conflict that was sure as tomorrow. An air of expectancy permeated the camps. Horses were fed, guns were cleaned, points for arrows and lances struck, and guns tested. Sitting Bull scented soldiers trailing him; still no one was visibly frightened. And in increasing repugnance was instilling a hemorrhaging crescendo in warrior anxiety. A formidable fighting force of seasoned warriors was ready for instant action. And didn't they have the superstrategist, Sitting Bull, as their leader? Wasn't he the cleverest tactician on the Great Plains? Time and again he agonized, "Even a bird will fight to defend its nest!"

The battle with "Three Stars" Crook has been fought about a week earlier. The military took enough beating to send other units into the field to strike the Indians down; thus more fighting was inevitable. "Soldiers keep coming to Sioux grounds like they fall from the sky!" Sitting Bull said sadly. Yet he was confident his side would win.

The head chief's lodge stood on the southwest side of the Hunkpapa circle on land about ten feet higher than the others. He studied the lowland to the north now covered with lodges and saw smoke from their wood and bison-chip fires spiraling into the sky. To the south, open flatland was visible through which the river years ago flowed eastward before changing again to a northward course. Dry, this old riverbed with high banks could serve as a defensive trench. To the west guarded ponies grazed unconcernedly on grass-covered benches. In the distance southward, the Big Horn Mountains stood tall. But Sitting Bull wanted a better view of the camp to fine-tune his plans and review his defensive strategy if the military should charge the camp. Limping up the low hill, he obtained the view he wanted. Afar he saw barren hills in the background; green timber to the east adorned the bottomland along the Little Big Horn. Interfering with the quiet of evening came the faint sound of drumming, singing, and all the natural noises of a huge gathering. Darkness slowly settled. Glowworms spotlighted their presence to each other and floated lazily about. Coyotes sang a happy introduction to night.

Sitting Bull, as usual, exhibited utmost confidence in the future. Hadn't he saved his people from being subjugated by enemy tribes and the military? Though he took grave chances himself, rarely did he apply this principle to his people, who were confident their head chief would not gamble and deploy a warrior assemblage of marginal capability and doubtful survivability. When families were involved, he always played it safe, and for their added protection

Sitting Bull—leader extraordinary.

Courtesy of the National Archives. CDR U.S. Army Audio Visual Center, MOAV-PL, Room 5A470, Pentagon.

at night, he ordered ponies tied to the lodges of their owners. Wasn't this planning for a sudden attack from the military? Yet he had the feeling his people were very much alone, so asked for help from above! Raising his arms in darkness, he pleaded with Wakan' Tanka, "I beg of you. Take pity. We want to live. Guard us from misfortune!"

And where was Gen. "Long Hair" Custer at this time? On the trail of these very Sioux, but still miles away. Talking to one group of his Indian scouts, he ordered them to steal the Sioux ponies. "You do this and I will look out for you when I come to power," he promised. Little did "Long Hair" know how carefully Sioux ponies were being guarded. Later Custer revealed to his Ree scouts something he had told no one else. "Everything is being staked on this coming battle with Sitting Bull," he warned "and I want to win big."

Later that night, Ree scouts, who reconnoitered the Sioux-Cheyenne camp, met with Custer. "Camp big," they told him. "End no seen. Ponies tied to lodges, guarded by young warriors ready for fight." Then the head Ree scout spoke. "More Indians in camp than you can handle," he forewarned Custer. But the general did not believe him. As he had been a daring victorious commander in the War between the States, he wondered, how could "savages" who never read the military manual fight on equal terms with people who had? But Indian fighting was new to Custer, and he overlooked one significant point. Sioux and Cheyenne, extraordinary horsemen and good shots, knew how to fight and fight fiercely—never once giving thought to their own safety. As a warrior band was overpowered, the horsemen faded away, giving the enemy a false sense of security. When the military stopped chasing them, they turned their ponies and made another furious charge, completely surprising the enemy. At times things got so confusing to white soldiers, they didn't know who was chasing who.

Came the night of June 24, 1876. General Custer and his seventh Cavalary rode the darkness through to reach the Indian camp. Custer sometimes was adorned in gold spurs taken from a fallen southern officer, but on this occasion the flamboyant leader was dressed plainly in blue-gray shirt, buckskin trousers, and high boots. A wide-brimmed hat rested firmly on his long yellow hair. He sat his horse erect. Every inch of him exhibited confidence. Though yet in his twenties, he was now brevet major general.

Custer's Seventh Cavalry was but one segment of the military force Brig. Gen. Alfred H. Terry, who commanded the entire operation, had arranged to attack the Sioux. Terry planned well. Custer would move his Seventh Cavalry along the Rosebud River, follow the Indian trail, send scouts ahead, but would keep the main body of his force, about six hundred troopers, behind. Employing this strategy, Custer would prevent Sitting Bull's warriors, when attacked by another unit of Terry's force, from escaping between the Little Big Horn Mountains and the river of the same name. Custer's march, if taken as directed, would give the other military force time to cross the Yellowstone River near the mouth of the Big Horn and move upstream toward Custer's unit. Sitting Bull then would be trapped between the forces on June 26. But Custer disregarded orders and attacked the Sioux camp on June 25, a day early.

So back to Custer! Traveling hard, his tired troopers halted for a few moments' rest in darkness early the morning of June 25, while his Indian scouts rode ahead to the top of Crow's Nest, a high point overlooking the Little Big Horn Valley. After this pause, march was resumed. At dawn the scouts and Custer assembled again. The sharp-eyed scouts reported seeing about ten miles away in faint moonlight the biggest herd of ponies they had ever seen, with most of them tied to the lodgepoles of tepees. Unknown to the scouts and partly concealed by summer haze, the might of the Sioux nation and its allies was encamped, some twelve thousand Indians. The United States Army expected to face fewer than one thousand warriors. Instead, Custer's troopers battled twice that number.

At the Sioux camp the day dawned bright and clear. The sun beat hot; the wind was down. It was June 25, 1876. No rain had fallen for weeks. Trails in every direction were thick with dust. At daybreak ponies were led to drink the cold water of the Little Big Horn. It took the Cheyennes, whose home territory was the southern plains, a good hour to water their many horses. Living near Mexico, they had more horses than the Sioux, many more. Two Moon, for instance, had twice as many as Sitting Bull. But Sitting Bull kept no large herd. He was always giving horses to poor members of the tribe.

Custer's Indian scouts the previous night had inspected the Sioux camp well. They stood convinced that General "Longhair" was hypnotized with excessive optimism as he faced a powerful

Indian force geared for battle. They warned him that defeat was possible. Bloody Knife, an Arikara scout and a wise old warrior, told him there were more braves in the Sioux camp than there were cartridges in the soldiers' belts. Looking at the rising sun, he whispered, "I shall not see you go down tonight!" Another scout was so pessimistic about victory he gave away everything in his "war sack." To them, the land itself was sending out distress signals.

But none of these warnings deterred Custer. He decided to attack as soon as he could reach the Sioux camp, actually a day earlier than General Terry ordered, thus without assistance from the other military units. Splitting his regiment into three battalions, he gave three companies to Maj. Marcus A. Reno, three to Capt. Fred W. Benteen, five to himself and assigned one company to guard the pack train. Benteen was ordered to bear left and scout the bluffs. If no Indians were found, he should follow the valley beyond. The rest of Custer's force would move northward down the stream called Reno Creek today. Reno was ordered to attack the camp from its southern end—a daring undertaking by any stretch of the imagination. Custer himself would take the remainder of the regiment across the Little Big Horn River, circle the huge encampment then recross the stream and attack from the north. On paper the maneuver, if properly coordinated, looked proper—Reno attack from the south and Custer from the north.

And what was happening at the Indian camp? Word of the approach of Major Reno's force came to Sitting Bull during an emergency meeting in the council lodge. Springing to his feet, throwing the bison-hide doorflap open, he ran to his own lodge nearby. Shouting that the camp was being attacked, he pointed southward up the river. Dust from the approaching troopers was slowly drifting upward. Soon the heads of horses and blue shirts of soldiers pierced the dust fog. Puffs of smoke from military carbines mushroomed into the lazy air, and reports from their weapons belatedly followed.

Now in his lodge, Sitting Bull grabbed his forty-five caliber pistol in one hand and his late-model Winchester .44 carbine in the other and rushed outside to stop the military tide. One Bull, his nephew, was bent on the same errand. Knowing his single-shot muzzle-loader would be useless against repeating rifles, he grabbed his stone-headed war club instead. Just then a bullet pierced the bison-hide tepee and shattered a lodgepole on the opposite side, barely missing him. "Uncle," he shouted, "I am going to meet the soldiers!" Sitting Bull, now ordering warrior leaders to specific positions shouted back, "Go at them, fear nothing," while throwing the carrying strap of his own bull bison-hide war shield over his nephew's head. Old men, boys and women with practiced speed hurriedly untied ponies so armed warriors could mount them quickly and be off. Buckling cartridge belt around his waist, Sitting Bull leaped on his favorite black steed and raced toward the charging cavalry.

In a sense, confusion in camp reigned for an instant, although from a defensive standpoint this is not a far appraisal. Men were ready. So were their ponies. Warriors everywhere, grabbing whatever weapons they owned, jumped on their horses and joined the charge. Old men shouted advice. Dogs running hither and yon were in everyone's way. Grabbing bows and arrows, young women with aged warriors formed a second line of defense. Elderly women, slow afoot, rounded up the children and ushered them away to hiding places in the wooded bottomland. Those who remained in camp secreted themselves ready to drive an arrow through any soldier who broke through the front line.

Chief Four Horns, Sitting Bull's uncle, old as he was, mounted his spotted bay and roan pony and hurried to battle, armed with a bow and quiverful of arrows. None of these metal firearms that shoot lead for him! An old master with bow and arrow, he could shoot with the best. Every Hunkpapa warrior now was mounted and was charging toward the oncoming cavalry. At the front the low bellow of Sitting Bull, shouting orders to his warriors could be heard: "Be brave. Keep moving. Charge in and out. Let no soldier through!"

And what did Major Reno and his advancing cavalry do when they left Custer? Following orders, Reno and his troopers moved at a bridle-jingling trot. Nearing the Sioux camp, it was his soldiers who encountered this hurricane of charging Hunkpapa horsemen armed with an assortment of weapons—rifles, lances, bows, arrows, and war clubs. As the military approached, the warrior avalanche hit them like a tornado. The first band quickly retreated, and immediately another group struck. Led by Sitting Bull, charge after charge followed. The military saw a virtuoso at work. So heavy was

Indian Warfare, by Frederic Remington.
Courtesy of the Thomas Gilcrease Institute of American History and Art, Tulsa, Oklahoma.

the attack, Reno dispersed his troopers and had them form a line across the valley. Absorbing no end of punishment, he then ordered his cavalrymen to dismount and fight on foot, with every fourth man holding the horses, But the ping-ping of bullets striking everywhere and the wave of arrows coming from nowhere frightened the animals. Many broke loose and escaped.

Reno's tactics puzzled Sitting Bull. Instead of Reno using his depleting cavalry in a charge attempt, the only way he could fight his way through, he had his men dismount and fight on foot. It must be said here that Reno was new to fighting Indians and, to put it charitably, looked the part. In his present predicament, he wondered why Custer was not attacking from the opposite end of camp. And where was Custer? At this very time he was skirting the bluffs on the east side of the Little Big Horn River, expecting to cross the stream and attack the camp from the north.

What Custer did not know was that the camp extended along the river for three miles. Furthermore, his was a winding route—trying not to be seen. All this maneuvering took time, too much time. Actually Reno's and Custer's planned attack was improperly coordinated. And Reno's battle tactics, so successful in the War between the States, proved impotent when fighting Plains Indians who charge in, veer off and then immediately regroup for another charge.

Seeing Reno's soldiers dismount, Sitting Bull was confident his camp with its women, old folks, and children was safe. So he ordered the warriors not only to attack the enemy from the front, but to strike it from all sides. No longer was it necessary for the Hunkpapa to remain between the soldiers and camp—the cavalrymen were going nowhere. Like starving prairie wolves attacking a bison yearling, warriors swarmed around Reno's bluecoats, torturing them from the front, flanking them from the sides, and running them down from the rear. The sweet aroma of success was whetting an insatiable appetite. No retreat now was open to the soldiers. Forced into a cottonwood grove, the remaining troopers took refuge behind the high banks of the old river channel.

But Sitting Bull, the grizzled head chief—the Soul of the Old West—too shrewd and battle-wise to underestimate the striking power of an enemy, was worried. Wasn't Reno employing peculiar strategy? Something was up. Was the military leader setting a trap? Concernedly, Sitting Bull alerted his warriors, shouting "Be careful.

There is some trick about this. Watch behind you!"

Meanwhile, One Bull, the Head Chief's nephew, became indoctrinated with the battle spirit. Wearing the shield hurriedly thrown over his shoulder by Sitting Bull, he participated in every alternate charge. Shields were effective protection, except for direct rifle hits, used in front of their bodies during a charge and behind their bodies during each temporary retreat. In an awesome display of power, warriors continued pouring bullets and arrows into the dwindling military ranks. But the soldiers, though substantially outnumbered now, had marksmen also. Black Moon was shot from his horse. Mortally wounded, he cheered the others on while the bullet drained his life. Then Good Bear Boy went down and White Bull was killed. Warriors fell repeatedly, and the battle continued.

Sitting Bull decided he had the answer to Reno's tactics. The commander was waiting for another body of soldiers in accordance with a prearranged plan. There *was* another military unit around! So the head chief ordered his best scouts to scour the countryside and find it. Those selected galloped off while the remaining warriors continued to thrash the enemy. Reno's success now became treacherously thin. Soon the battle became an utter rout, due primarily to Custer disobeying his military orders but also to Reno's inexperienced leadership in Indian warfare. After the Battle of the Little Big Horn, Cheyenne warriors said it was bad luck for Reno that he hit the Hunkpapa Sioux camp first. Actually he attacked the best-trained and fiercest Indian warriors of the day—led by the clever tactician Sitting Bull himself.

During this raging battle, where was Captin Benteen? Discovering no Indians along the route assigned him, he headed back to the Indian trail that Reno followed. There he met trumpeter John Martin carrying this urgent message: "Benteen, come on. Big village. Be quick. Bring ammunition packs." So Benteen hastened onward. When the roll of gunfire and war whoops struck him, he assumed it was Custer being attacked. Hurrying on, he learned it was Reno battling Sitting Bull's Hunkpapa. In no time he too was surrounded. Though Benteen's three companies prolonged the battle, they did little to change its tide. One soldier fell, then another, and his fighting force declined catastrophically. Before long the Hunkpapa warriors bathed in glory. The military units on the south front had been wiped out. Yet the high banks of the old river channel stood mute, silently guarding the tragic story of those killed there.

Reno's tactics kept gnawing on Sitting Bull. Seeing the military force dismount during the heat of battle, the head chief fully expected a charge from the rear. It never came. With Reno's and Benteen's forces destroyed, Sitting Bull headed for his village. It was deserted save for old folks and those who formed the second line of defense. Rushing forward, they greeted him warmly. Almost exhausted, his voice spent from shouting orders, he reached the semideserted village. Sitting his black pony, he saw the women and children come out of hiding in the wooded river bottomland. Proud he was that the young boys helped women keep children well concealed.

Just then one of Sitting Bull's scouts riding a horse white with sweat slid to a stop in front of him. "Big enemy across river!" he shouted. Then a second scout on a winded pony brought the same news. Here was the answer to Sitting Bull's puzzle. Major Reno *was* expecting help from another military force—troopers planning to strike the camp from the rear. It was General Custer himself, with five companies of cavalrymen. That was why Reno's men dismounted, fought on foot behind the high banks of Little Big Horn's old channel in the cottonwood grove, and waited!

And where was Custer when Reno and his men were fighting for their very lives? As prearranged, his force was double-timing it northward, skirting knolls—traveling about a mile inland from the Little Big Horn River. Custer was attempting to reach the north end of the giant camp, following his own ill-conceived plan. He would attack from the rear the Indians fighting Reno. But he never made it! Cheyenne and Oglala scouts stationed at high points round about telegraphed messages by mirror flashes to Chief Crazy Horse, the crafty combatant guarding the north end of camp while Sitting Bull protected the south. Although Crazy Horse surmised Custer's strategy, he would not commit his warriors to battle until he knew exactly where the general would approach the Oglala encampment.

Custer moved stealthily, skirting the back side of a low ridge toward the Cheyenne and Oglala tepees. When Crazy Horse decided he knew enough of Custer's plans, he moved to attack, but only after maneuvering to get the sun to his advantage—an old Indian trick! At first only a few warriors charged the cavalry column, then wave after wave, with the sun to their backs, came. Soon the prairie was alive with moving horsemen. Attacked, Custer looked about for a more suitable fighting location. Could his troopers make it to that knoll over there? No, they could not! Little did he know he was on the brink of infamy! Mounted Cheyennes and Oglalas now charged from front and rear, then came from everywhere. Crazy Horse gave no mercy—he in turn expected none. His warriors, smelling victory, charged in, emptying their guns, shooting a blast of arrows, throwing their lances into the ranks of the cavalry, then wildly riding away. And as every leader knows, once fighting men "smell" victory they are unbeatable. Yet the troopers, fighting like cornered wildcats, fought unyieldingly.

Despite the encirclement, Custer penetrated the Indian line and obtained possession of a nearby knoll. But then he made a fatal mistake, the same as Reno made earlier, by employing strategy used

U.S. MILITARY ATTACK ON SIOUX AND ALLIES CAMP

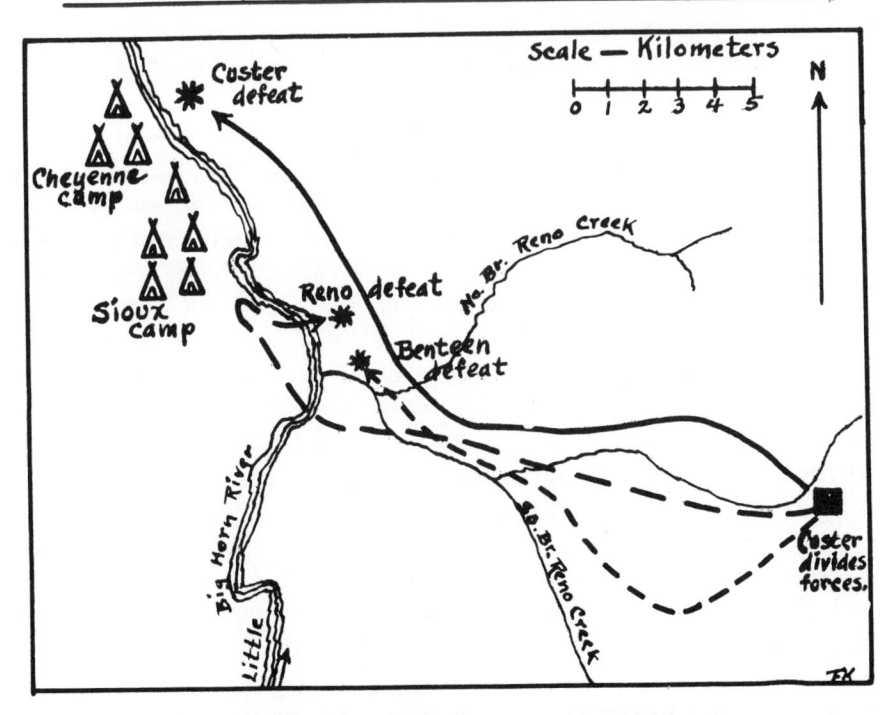

ROUTES BY CUSTER ———, RENO — —, BENTEEN — — —.

successfully in the War between the States. Dismounting, he grouped his troopers in a compact circle of resistance. But soon he realized he was fighting a different enemy. Like a prairie tornado, mounted warriors charged in, fired, then charged out. Now Hunkpapa from the south front arrived and joined the attack. During each assault more soldiers fell. Working with Crazy Horse was Chief Gall, another warrior of renown, simultaneously storming the troopers at the lower edge of the hill.

Smoke from carbine fire and dust kicked up by the Indian ponies choked the stationary cavalrymen. Black as night the day turned! Soldiers were unable to see the mounted warriors charging in and out, but Crazy Horse's riders knew where the whites were huddled and kept pouring bullets and arrows into the mass of humanity. Noise from the battle blended into a roar like Niagara Falls. Sounds of war whoops and gun blasts chilled the air. Then all hell broke loose! The ground shook. Soldiers hit while standing fell backward—those kneeling fell on their faces. Dead and wounded, soldiers, Indians, horses, covered the ground, which turned red. Yet, more warriors joined in the attack. As one fell, two took his place.

Running short on ammunition, Benteen's ammunition train could be the difference between victory and defeat. Custer began to wonder whether his urgent message reached the captain. Custer of course did not know that Benteen was fighting for his very life at the opposite end of camp three miles away. Benteen already had so many problems, if a new one surfaced it would be days before he could consider it.

Sensing that ammunition was running short, inasmuch as less carbine fire came from Custer's cavalrymen, Crazy Horse and his crack warriors charged in closer, expecting to finish off the troopers. But the few remaining cavalrymen had other ideas! With carbines now empty they took to their pistols—weapons small but deadly at close range. Wave after wave of the charging warriors was repelled. Feeling the painful bite of the small weapons spitting death, the Indians retreated for a moment and regrouped. Then, and not until then, when smoke and dust cleared, did Custer realize his hopelessness. Completely surrounded by hundreds of anxious Indians, he saw little chance of victory. Still confident to the last, brave soldier that he was, he stood erect, shouting orders to his men now firing from kneeling position, simultaneously feeling the cartridge belt for more ammunition for his pistol. It wasn't there. Another soldier, mortally wounded, crawled over the dead and handed his commander the few remaining cartridges he had. "Easy on the ammunition!" shouted Custer. "Make every shot count!" Exhausted from the all-night travel and the grueling battle, his men gave no response. The physical expenditure and lack of water had drained their energy. Throats were parched and burning. The wounded bandaged themselves the best they could with cloth torn from their own uniforms or lay unattended under the boiling sun. Custer's vision of a big victory—any victory—was shattered.

And the battle continued. Soon pistol chambers as well as rifle barrels of the military were empty. Ammunition was gone! Still the troops would not capitulate—what was left of them! Hand-to-hand fighting grew fierce, with cavalrymen using their carbines as clubs. But the battle couldn't last, and it didn't. Soon all was quiet. Custer and his soldiers were annihilated to the man. Around Custer's body, which lay just short of the crest of the hill he so desperately needed and which Crazy Horse denied him, lay his closest comrades—his two brothers, Tom and Benton Custer, and Autie Reed and Calhoun. It was four o'clock in the afternoon. Reno and Benteen had been silenced more than an hour earlier. Thus General Custer and his six hundred-man Seventh Calvalry, an additional four hundred-man infantry, as well as numerous loyal Indian scouts who warned him defeat was inevitable, met death after a violent, exhaustive battle.

If this encounter was not the most tenacious military battle ever fought on American soil, and warfare historians treasure the War between the States past with reverence, it surely ranks as the most devastating—every American soldier fought to the death, not one living soldier remained.

No reason was given by the victorious Indians to single out any soldier as the bravest, but they did. One trooper the warriors admired, whom they named bravest of all. He wore three stripes on his sleeve. With ammunition spent, he ran to one side and, by swinging his carbine with all the force his overworked body could mobilize, fought off several attacking Indians singlehandedly for a time. His uniform, red with blood, was torn to shreds. The man was Sergeant Butler. Yes, the warriors agreed, he was the bravest

Attack of the Wagon Train (anonymous).

trooper. So the U.S. military was not without its heroes, but heroism in a losing effort seldom is rewarded.

While the battle between Crazy Horse and General Custer raged, Sitting Bull took no chances, forming a second line of defense at the Cheyenne and Oglala circle of lodges. Crazy Horse rode twice to Sitting Bull for hurried counsel. When the din of battle echoed into the distance, the head chief rode across the river. "Are they all killed?" he asked a returning warrior. "Yes!" was the reply. Chiefs Sitting Bull and Crazy Horse and several warriors went to view those lying on the field of battle. They looked at Custer, whom they respected as a brave soldier. "If that is Long Hair, with my war club I killed him as I raced by pony through their center," the young nephew of Sitting Bull volunteered when Bad Juice pointed to Custer's body. The Battle of Little Big Horn, designed to wipe Sitting Bull off the face of the earth, was over. But the Indian victory dance was postponed, as too many warriors had fallen for anyone to rejoice. And those who survived were near collapse from the paralyzing combat. Following Sioux custom, prairie grass at several points was set afire in the distance. Its huge smoke clouds, visible for miles, telegraphed a smashing victory. Again Sitting Bull, the old fox, had won over the might of the military. His superb qualities of warfare excellence would well merit him the designation Warrior of the Century.

In death General Custer, through a tempestuous demonstration of bravery, achieved the historical immortality for which he yearned, but in its wake the lives of many soldiers were sacrificed. President Grant, a general of distinction, summed up the Little Big Horn battle in *the Army and Navy Journal* this way: "I regard Custer's massacre as a sacrifice of troops, brought on by himself, that was wholly unnecessary. He was not to have made the attack, but effect the juncture with Terry and Gibbon. He was told to meet them on the 26th, but instead of marching slowly as his orders required in order to effect the juncture on the 26th, he entered on a forced march of eighty-three miles in twenty-four hours, and thus had to meet the Indians alone on the 25th."

An old mountain-man beaver trapper who had no part in the conquest, but who knew the Plains Indians well, appraised the battle this way: "Too many Indians—good shots, excellent riders, and the best fighters the sun ever shone on!"

Although Sitting Bull won the Battle of Little Big Horn, just as he won every battle while chief, this did not necessarily win the war. Military units took after him like yellow jackets flushed from their nest, and he finally left American soil for Canada. His strategy? To reorganize his braves and return to subdue the powerful military.

Sitting Bull, however, was unprepared for the harsh north prairieland. Wild prairie fires destroyed needed forage for Sioux pony herds, and deep snow along with extreme cold killed many animals. Human food during the long winter was virtually unavailable as bison began their southward migration early in the autumn. Severe famine weakened the people and struck them down. Distressingly, Sitting Bull made his decision. He would return to the United States and surrender, which he felt was best for his people, who were hungry and sick.

High noon, July 19, 1881, the distinguished chief and a few warriors of his tribe came to Fort Buford. "He wore plain clothes and did not appear to be a well man, showing in his face and figure the ravages of worry and hunger he had gone through," wrote a military officer. Thus Sitting Bull, who had been a hero to the Sioux nation since boyhood, was getting old and suffering. Definitive capitulation of his cherished independence was the final blow to his pride.

After surrendering, Sitting Bull calmy but firmly stated his feelings to the assembled officers: "The land I have under my feet is ours. I have never sold it. I never gave it to anybody. When I left the Black Hills five winters ago, it was because I wished to raise my Sioux people quietly . . . "

Totally broken, the illustrious chief felt surrender deeply. With Sioux freedom crushed, the powerful and respected Sioux thus completed their trail of no return.

VIII

Mystery of the Indian Mounds

Of all archaeological remains that tantalized white man, Indian mounds were the most challenging. Someone built them, but who? They were built long ago, but when? Something could be in them, but what?

For years an aura of mystery hung over the builders of these earth mounds. At first they were considered a superior race of prehistoric people of high culture—a race that came as mysteriously as it vanished. Now it is believed Indians of succeeding cultures built these earthworks over a period of centuries. Earliest mounds date from about the birth of Christ, the latest at the time Europeans came to settle North America.

Dr. David Baerreis, professor of anthropology at the University of Wisconsin-Madison, believes burials had been placed in all mounds. Nor does the fact that some yielded no discernible skeletal remains move him from this belief. "I have a feeling," he relates, "that a chemical analysis of the soil at the proper spot in these mounds would reveal a higher than normal content of phosphorus, calcium, and the like, indicating a human being had been buried in the mound." Skeletal remains, Dr. Baerreis relates, can be detected better in some soil and moisture types than in others.

Seen by early whites who settled along the eastern seaboard were strange earthen mounds. Later they learned the mounds extended westward to the Mississippi River and beyond. Ranging from hardly perceptible humps on the ground surface to hillocks thirty feet high, some covered an acre or more. As many as one hundred thousand mounds may have been built in these United States before an expanding white population began their mass destruction. But the mounds were unmistakable evidence that far into the past people lived and died on this land.

Courtesy of the Milwaukee Public Museum

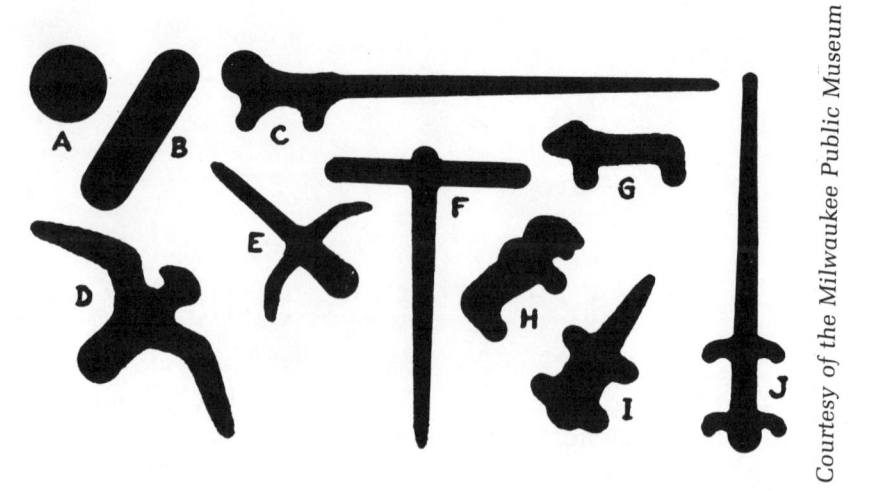

Effigy mound shapes: A. Conical, B. Linear, C. Panther, D. Eagle, E. Goose, F. Bird, G. Bear, H. Bison, I. Turtle, J. Lizard.

Earliest earthen mounds apparently were monuments to honor the dead. Such lasting memorials were not restricted to North America. They were worldwide. Races in early days felt they were showing the greatest respect to someone whose loss bore upon everyone alike. An earthen monument was erected so every person, including the most humble, could pay silent tribute to the deceased relative or friend. Nothing, they believed, was more enduring than a mound of earth. Through vicissitudes of time, it would remain unchanged while any other product of human effort would be reduced to ruins.

An Indian warrior who would track a deer twenty miles or walk a hundred miles to ambush an enemy, or a woman who would work days tanning hides surely would be willing to help build a mound to honor a chieftain or relative at death. They could display their grief and respect by carrying a few animal hides or baskets of soil and depositing it over the deceased.

Take the Cahokia mounds! Scientists report they required one thousand persons five years to erect, with the means at their command. And from the structures of soil and stone created over this nation by prehistoric inhabitants, surely they possessed appreciable genius and engineering skill. Nothing, it seems, was too great an effort to commemorate their distinguished dead. The same held true for purposes of worship or for preparing places of safety when imperiled. In these categories they exhibited an intensity of zeal and consecreation that have few parallels. In mounds for burials they demonstrated a love and veneration for their dead that have infrequent equals in the annals of mankind.

Two types of mounds are most common: 1) conical or linear and 2) effigy. A conical mound required an estimated fifty cubic yards of earth. It could be easily erected by twenty-five persons in one day. A linear mound, depending upon its length and height, required substantially more soil and greater effort. An effigy mound demanded engineering and art designs beyond the ordinary. Building it invited communal effort: perhaps the entire Indian band participated. A bear effigy 80 feet long, 20 feet wide, and four feet high might require 250 cubic yards of soil and take 125 persons to build in a day.

Scientists today believe they know who built these mounds. They were constructed by ancestors of modern Indians. The variations of shape, size, and content suggest that many tribes, not just one, built them—not at the same time nor even within a period of a hundred years. Nor were the builders at the same state of cultural development.

Mounds, of course, vary as much in their internal features as in their external shape. Dead in some were placed in shallow pits dug into undisturbed soil. In others, burials were laid on the ground and earth was placed over them. And the treatment of bodies before burial varied. Some were buried in their flesh, others with no flesh on their bones—the bundle burial. In this latter instance the body was exposed to the air until the flesh was gone—then bones were gathered, combined into a bundle, and buried.

Hopewell Indians built conical mounds that contained several corpses deposited over a period of years, and their grave offerings were something beautiful and useful. Included were pearl and copper beads, decorated clay pots, large stone spearheads and knives, and copper breastplates. Bodies of some persons were wrapped in native plant-fiber cloth with the material preserved through chemical action unto this day, especially where the fiber pressed against copper objects. This Hopewell culture covered much of the Midwest from about A.D. 900 to A.D. 1300.

Effigy mounds are a select class. Built in shapes of animals and birds, they are centered in Wisconsin, southeastern Minnesota, the eastern fringe of Iowa, and northwestern Illinois. Indians of North American may have built conical and linear earthworks first; then later certain bands developed a distinct Effigy Mound Culture with their corresponding earthworks in shapes of animals and birds, one chosen as representing their particular clan. While these earthworks were built chiefly for ceremonial and religious functions, in many cases and perhaps all important members of the clan were buried. Most students of the subject believe the Effigy Mound culture reached its artistic peak from A.D. 500 to A.D. 1200, beginning somewhat earlier than the Hopewell culture.

And what happened to the Effigy Mound people? Perhaps they were attacked by invading enemies and their culture destroyed, but more likely they were absorbed by other tribes with different beliefs.

Two prehistoric mound types and one village of special interest will be described here. Included are the Dickson Mound in Dickson Mounds State Park, the village of Aztalan in Aztalan State Park, and effigy mounds in Effigy Mounds National Monument.

Linear Type: Dickson Mound in Northern Illinois

Five hundred and fifty feet long, standing twenty-five above the ground surface at its highest point, the Dickson Mound lies near the Illinois and Spoon rivers. It may have been a burial ground for a hundred years. Excavated by scientists, 230 skeletons were found in a space thirty by sixty feet. Lying exactly as buried, the skeletons, along with their many utility and ornament pieces, now are exposed to view. Protected by a large shelter building, today persons can view skeletons and artifacts in their original position, readily available for observation and study. Such a large number of burials grouped together raises an interesting point of conjecture. Judging from the condition of the skeletons, war was not the cause of death. Death by pestilence is the most logical.

Burials over decades followed no set pattern. After death each body was laid upon the ground surface or placed in a pit and covered with soil, burying one over another until a large mound was built. After a time, skeletons extended from top to base and from one side to the other. Burials were made in a way that the people surely believed in a future existence. With a tiny babe a small piece of pottery, probably filled with food, was placed along with beads and a Gulf of Mexico shell pendant. Although the babe was too young to use the articles, the family believed the child would need them at a later date.

Much of the family life and culture of these Indians is reflected in their burials. Not a single artifact shows contact with the white race. Apparently these people came to Illinois from the south, pushing away those who were living on the land at the time. The famous Cahokia Mounds in southern Illinois have much in common with the Dickson Mound, and quite possibly the people migrated from there. The people represent a late period of the Middle phase of the Mississippi Culture. Burials in the Dickson Mound were made between six hundred and one thousand years ago.

Everything points to a peaceful people who had tremendous respect and feeling for one another. They lived in small villages with rectangular houses set in bowl-shaped depressions, and much of their food included native animals: deer, elk, bison, and small game. But as they were agriculturally oriented, maize, beans, squash, and other foods they raised were an important part of their diet.

Village Type: Aztalan in Southern Wisconsin

A band of Indians living in the southern part of our nation journeyed up the Mississippi River, settling about where East Saint Louis, Illinois, stands today. Here they established Cahokia, the largest known prehistoric complex north of Central Mexico. After a time, a group from this band with an established Middle Mississippi culture made its way northward—eventually along the Rock River and finally up its tributary, the Crawfish. Along the west bank of this stream in today's Jefferson county, Wisconsin, the colony settled, living for about a hundred years on products they grew, animals killed, and fish caught. The time? About nine hundred years ago, presumably between A.D. 1075 and 1175. By the time European explorers appeared on the horizon, the band had disappeared, leaving no clue to its fate.

Aztalan village—an artist's reconstruction showing the twelve-foot-high log stockade, with defense towers at about eighty-foot intervals, large pyramidal mounds at the far corners, houses, and a field of maize in the center.

Courtesy of the Milwaukee Public Museum.

The village, when inhabited, was a stockade surrounded by walls about fifteen feet high. Upright poles with clay packed between made the thick walls a formidable barrier to local Indian enemies. Not a single stockade, it was partitioned into three, forming a carefully arranged protective system for the residences and maize field within. The maize was the twelve-row variety, similiar to that grown at Cahokia. Abutments and watchtowers were stationed at regular intervals.

Prominent within the stockade were two large pyramidal mounds and a central platform. The earthen mound in the southwest corner, sixty by sixty-five feet at the top, larger at the base, apparently was surrounded by a lesser stockade of poles. A similar mound in the northwest corner, truncated, without terraces, was somewhat smaller. A high platform stood on a still smaller mound near the center of the east portion of the village. Inasmuch as the two large mounds appeared similar to Aztec temple mounds of Mexico, Judge N. F. Hyer, an early settler, and Timothy Johnson, who discovered and reported the village remains in 1836, believed it was the original homeland of the Aztecs. Thus Judge Hyer named the village Aztalan and hastily surveyed the village enclosure. He published his findings in 1837 in the *Greenwich Eagle*, a newspaper in New York State. *The Milwaukee Advertiser*, Wisconsin's only newspaper, reprinted the account on February 26, 1837.

Not until 1850 was any serious attempt made to investigate the site further and record the findings. First to do this was Dr. Increase A. Lapham, with some financial assistance from the American Antiquarian Society. Lapham's discoveries were published in 1855, titled *Antiquities of Wisconsin,* and are Volume 7 in *Smithsonian Contributions to Knowledge.*

When a person or even a group of persons attempts to preserve a historic site, untold difficulties arise. Take the case of Aztalan Village. Within a year after the village ruins were discovered, Edward Everett, who recognized its historic value, attempted to preserve the site for future generations. Contacting President Van Buren, he urged him to withdraw from sale the section of public land on which the village was located, thus to save this historic site from further destruction. But nothing came of it! No sentiment favoring Everett's recommendation was aroused. The government sold the entire site to a private purchaser for a mere twenty-two dollars.

No further effort to preserve Aztalan was initiated until 1912, when local citizens became interested enough to raise funds through private contributions. Purchasing the burial mounds area at the top of the hill, they named it Mound Park. All the while the village site was being farmed and the large pyramidal mounds were wearing away. To hurry the process, horse-drawn scrapers were used to level the land and make it easier to crop. Finally, in 1919 and 1920, the Milwaukee Public Museum, under Dr. S. A. Barrett, began an extensive excavation and research investigation of the village remains. Appreciable data were obtained.

Of the original double rows of seventy-four conical mounds in the northwest corner, only ten remain. Fortunately in 1948, the 120 acres were acquired by the Wisconsin Conservation Department, today's Wisconin Department of Natural Resources, and named Aztalan State Park. The two pyramidal mounds in the southwest and northwest corners have been partially restored, as have portions of the stockade—using wooden poles set upright as in the original inclosure. Much of today's restoration is based on data obtained by Dr. Barrett and by the State Historical Society of Wisconsin. Several organizations contributed time, effort, and scientific knowledge to the restoration task. Included were the Lake Mills–Aztalan Historical Society, the Wisconin Archeological Society, the Milwaukee

Public Museum, the State Historical Society of Wisconsin, and private citizens.

But back to the early village of Aztalan! What was its population? No more than five hundred people, perhaps less. In arts and crafts the inhabitants were well advanced for the time, utilizing bone, shell, stone, horn, and wood. They lived on home-grown agricultural products, augmented with fish, mammals, birds, nuts, and berries. Their customs and ways of life, the design of the village, the use of pyramids for public functions, use of stone, knowledge of pottery, including ear spools, and their advanced art concepts indicate the people not only were different from the local Woodland Indians, but culturally much more advanced. The Aztalan people represented a high plane of living and a perceptive aristocracy from the deep south—a culture that had its impetus, directly or indirectly, from Indians within Mexico. And this culture, as it spread northward, mixed with local Woodland Indian tradition.

But why the people migrated to this site on the Crawfish River and built Aztalan village is not entirely clear. Perhaps this Aztalan site acted, in part, as a clearinghouse for trade goods from the northern regions.

Nothing has been found at Aztalan that would indicate the village was occupied for more than a century. Fire marks on the stockade remains and house walls have led scientists to conclude that Aztalan was burned by Indian enemies or by the inhabitants when they fled. Quite possibly these cultured people who moved into a territory controlled by warlike Woodland Indians and who excelled in everything but warfare were finally driven out, which accounts for their sudden disappearance.

Effigy Type: Effigy Mounds in Northeast Iowa

Beginning about A.D. 200, an exclusive Indian conglomerate for almost a thousand years built for ceremonial purposes low earthen mounds shaped like mammals and birds in which they buried a few distinguished members of their clan. Rarely more than four feet high, but sometimes five hundred feet or more in length, these mounds have aroused the curiosity and interest of people worldwide. Shapes of the mounds leave no doubt about what the people were trying to symbolize. Readily recognizable are the flying bird, panther, bear, and lizard, although only aerial views do them justice. Each effigy represents the clan symbol associated with the religious beliefs of the people. It invoked protection for the clan's superspirit and likely was used solely for ceremonials of serious nature.

Unique to the world, these silent effigy memorials are concentrated in the upper Mississippi River area, centering in southern Wisconsin and spilling over into nearby portions of Illinois, Iowa, and Minnesota. Occasional mounds have been found in Michigan and Ohio, but rarely in other states. Early white settlers in Wisconsin discovered effigy mounds in abundance, finding them in the Milwaukee and Waukesha areas, at Lake Geneva, at the four lakes around Madison, at Devil's Lake, at Green Lake, at Lake Winnebago, along the bluffs overlooking the Mississippi and Wisconsin rivers, and at other locations. Spectacular indeed is the huge bird mound on the state hospital grounds along the north shore of Lake Mendota at Madison, having a wingspread of 624 feet and being 6 feet high. At Buffalo Lake in Marquette County a panther mound is 575 feet long, including tail, and Man Mound near Baraboo, Wisconsin, representing a human being, originally was 214 feet long, but unfortunately the lower portion of its legs was removed during road construction.

Effigy mounds, oftentimes unrecognized by early settlers as man-made, have been destroyed by plow, scraper, and other means. Only an estimated one thousand undamaged earthworks remain. To preserve some as memorials of the Effigy Mound culture brought forth the establishment of Effigy Mounds National Monument in northeast Iowa, Lizard Mound State Park in southeast Wisconsin, and a few others.

Take the animal-shaped earthworks in Effigy Mounds National Monument, located in a region of secluded valleys and weatherworn bluffs along the Mississippi River. Here Indians of an effigy mound culture lived circa one thousand years ago. The culture was strangely simple, but it may be so only because we know so little about it. Nevertheless, the mystery slowly is unraveled by studying mounds and debris left at village sites. Although some early scientists attributed the earthworks to a mysterious race of Moundbuilders, today we know they were built by ancestors of our modern Indians. There is no "lost race" involved!

Effigy Mound culture apparently is an offshoot of the Hopewell

Indians, who gradually became dominant in the Midwest. Some scholars believe the culture Siouan in origin, inasmuch as it began in the Siouan section of Wisconsin—an area later occupied by their relatives the Winnebago and a few related tribes nearby. The people practiced a primitive agriculture, an indication that they had a high culture for the time. Although this implies a fair degree of social organization, their basic economy was limited. For food they hunted, fished, and gathered edible plants and nuts of prairie and woods. Animals for food included deer, elk, bear, bison, beaver, small game, turkey, grouse, swan, goose, and other bird life. Plant food included wild rice, oak acorns, hickory nuts, black walnuts, wild cherries, plums, grapes, maple syrup, and a variety of berries. They also may have grown maize. Returning from an autumn hunt, they probably harvested the maize and held a harvest ceremonial.

Effigy Mound people hunted principally with the bow and arrow and the spear. Animal snares and earth pits perhaps were used also. Fishing was done with harpoons, hooks of stone and copper, and net traps of plant fiber. Little is known of their houses, although they were temporary shelters—presumably huts of

A bobcat at rest.
Courtesy of the Wisconsin Department of Natural Resources.

wooden frame covered by hides and plates of tree bark. Cooking was done over a flame. Fired jar-shaped pottery vessels with broad tops were used when cooking foods containing liquids. At burial, small pots were placed beside the corpse, perhaps with food in them for later life. Their clay pipes imply that they had tobacco and probably smoked, not necessarily for pleasure, but during special occasions. Although clothed mostly in animal hides, they also had cloth—made from local plants. Bone and copper awls were used for sewing.

Burials for the rank-and-file Indians of the clan usually were made in conical or linear mounds or in unmarked graves near their village. Few of high rank were buried in the effigy mound representing their clan.

Why Effigy Mound people ceased building effigies is as much a mystery as the people themselves. This phase of their culture ceased long before the arrival of European settlers, and when whites asked historic Indians about the ancient mound builders, they had no knowledge of them.

Today there is little to remind us of the glory days of the mound builders except a few artifacts in museums and the remaining earthworks that survived the destructive force of modern man and time. While other nations boast of their spectacular archaeological remains, the United States takes pride in its effigy mounds, a unique treasure of the ancient Indian.

IX

Echoes of a Patriot

The warrior sleeps! Bow in hand he fell—silenced by an enemy arrow. But time moved onward. His wooden bow and buckskin quiver and arrows five decomposed. The stone points; color, size and shape similar, flaked by his own hands, lay together in a sand blowout along an ancient channel of the Fox River in Marquette County, Wisconsin, which no longer carries water. Ten inches away a point unlike the others lay. Was it the one that struck the fatal blow? Without question the five points, flaked before the birth of Christ, lay for centuries. Found together, presumably as they had been in the quiver, the author, who discovered the points, now has them in his collection.

What sparked this vicious conflict between tribes—if there was a conflict? Were they locked in battle over the control of this strategic water highway? With rivers being "interstate highways" at the time, any attempt by one tribe to restrict passage by others generated savage battles. Armed-to-the-teeth war parties, when challenged, fought their way through. Friendly tribes bent on trading with their neighbors could not. Conjecture leads one to believe our warrior fell while a battle of some proportion raged. Artifacts distributed over the wind-blown terrain testify that countless arrows and spears were released, presumably during the conflict. Even with Indian bodies stilled, ghosts of an earlier day reenacting the battle were envisioned when the artifacts strewn throughout the sand blowout were collected. And by listening closely, one could fancy hearing the whistling arrows cutting the air.

And our warrior is no more! Like others in those ancient times, he had no fear of death. To lose his life in battle brought fame and honor posthumously, and the years passed him by. During this period of unrecorded time, tree roots of the forest held the sandy

A man dwarfed by Wisconsin white pines.

Courtesy of the Wisconsin Department of Natural Resources.

soil together like talons of an eagle gripping a walleye. But then lightening struck and fire destroyed the forest. And the winds blew! With no trees to hold Mother Earth, sand blowouts pitted the landscape, uncovering evidence of a violent battle.

What generated this brutal disagreement at the Fox River? I would speculate that it was a power play between tribes. The stream was an impressive water highway—a highway linking the

Red fox—arch-schemer and trickster.

Great Lakes with the Gulf of Mexico. Traffic from Lake Michigan moved into Green Bay, then up Fox River, thence portaged a mile overland to the south-flowing Wisconsin River at a point where Portage, Wisconsin, stands today. Down the Wisconsin the canoes and dugouts were current-propelled to the mighty Mississippi and on to the Gulf of Mexico. So the Fox undoubtedly was an "interstate highway" between two great bodies of water—a travel route of extraordinary significance.

Was our warrior defending this water highway at a designated point? No written records tell the story, nor have hieroglyphic accounts of the battle been found carved on cliff walls. But ancient human hands left history—flaked stone points that whispered a voice of fact. So we know the approximate date of the confrontation. Through these finds, but more particularly through scientific excavation, historians piece the puzzle of human existence in North America. With this knowledge a better life is possible for those of us inhabiting the land today. But whether a better life has evolved remains unproven.

Farmers say the land is fertile now. And well it should be, having been watered by the blood of Indians for generations. Over centuries a legion of warriors fell in combat, leaving weapons of stone and copper on battlefields. Resisting destruction, those points portray an incomplete story of a civilization on this land long before white man. And if our warrior lived today, what would his future be? Like others of his noble race, he would be a man of destiny. The land he used judiciously and to which he claimed home but not ownership now is covered with cities, ranches, and farms. Without this vast reservoir of land on which to roam freely and hunt deer, bison, and other animals for food, he would be "fenced in" like a child in a playpen. Over the late years his only certainty has been uncertainty.

Today the American Indian realizes he has little influence or freedom on the land his ancestors entrusted to him and he so dearly loved, and his soul is slowly dying. His heart is forced away from a happy life close to this beloved nature and into strange, artificial surroundings. He is thrown into a totally unfamiliar world—a world of machines—and his tiring heart hangs to the world of yesterday, hoping for a miracle. Yet in his dreams—streams and lakes hugging wild rice stalks, bison pushing through ocean-wave prairie grass, and trees pressed against the earth's beloved breast—the friendly spirits of yesteryear never died!

The American Indian of today for the most part has become an object of white man's creation. He bears a white man's name, lives in white man's confined quarters, and watches himself on an unreal and confused version in television and motion pictures. He suffers along an endless road of rejection, and now nothing remains but the melting pot of races. If this fails, what will it be?

Let no one picture the ancient warrior as one without character. He fought endlessly to live his own life; the efforts ended in an

Courtesy of the Wisconsin Department of Natural Resources.

"Hey, Ma . . . wait for us!"

honorable death. Yet, like others over the years, those who fight hardest suffer the most. But do they? Our ancient warrior and others at the Fox River gave everything. Their voices are silent now, yet the stone artifacts they left behind relate the story of a civilization that survived untold centuries, but disappeared—along a trail of no return!

X

Contributions to Our Civilization

Pottery designs, basketry, cloth weaving, and ornament fashioning are but a few of the arts and crafts ancient Indians gave our civilization. Indian drama and dance, differing by tribes, are folk arts as distinctive as they are original, and the pioneering characteristics of these ancient Americans are inspiring traditions for us today. The daring feats of warriors of those days and the incomparable skills of the women provide modern youth with fitting examples of ingenuity and sophisticated human resourcefulness.

Take but one field—medicine. Settlers in early days who had no white physician nearby called the Indian medicine man to treat them, and several of the Indian treatments became recognized as effective cures. Not too strangely, many of the drugs and herbs the medicine man prescribed came into common use by grateful whites.

Today profound interest focuses on psychiatry and psychosomatic illnesses, and some of the studies center on why ancient Indian curers oftentimes restored health to sick Indians merely by bringing their mental state back into harmony with the natural environment. Thus several of these medicine man treatments are being studied anew by medical researchers. So, at long last, the medical profession is acknowledging a greater respect for some of these Indian-prescribed treatments.

Not many of us recognize or appreciate the endless contributions American Indians gave to our world. But medicine was a mere droplet of water into a pail overflowing. Ancient Indians gave generously in many fields, including agricultural products, arts, crafts, government, religion, family togetherness, rearing children, respect for the aged, and the feel for a natural environment. Let us meditate in silence upon this infinite generosity.

From the moment Europeans set foot on this continent, the

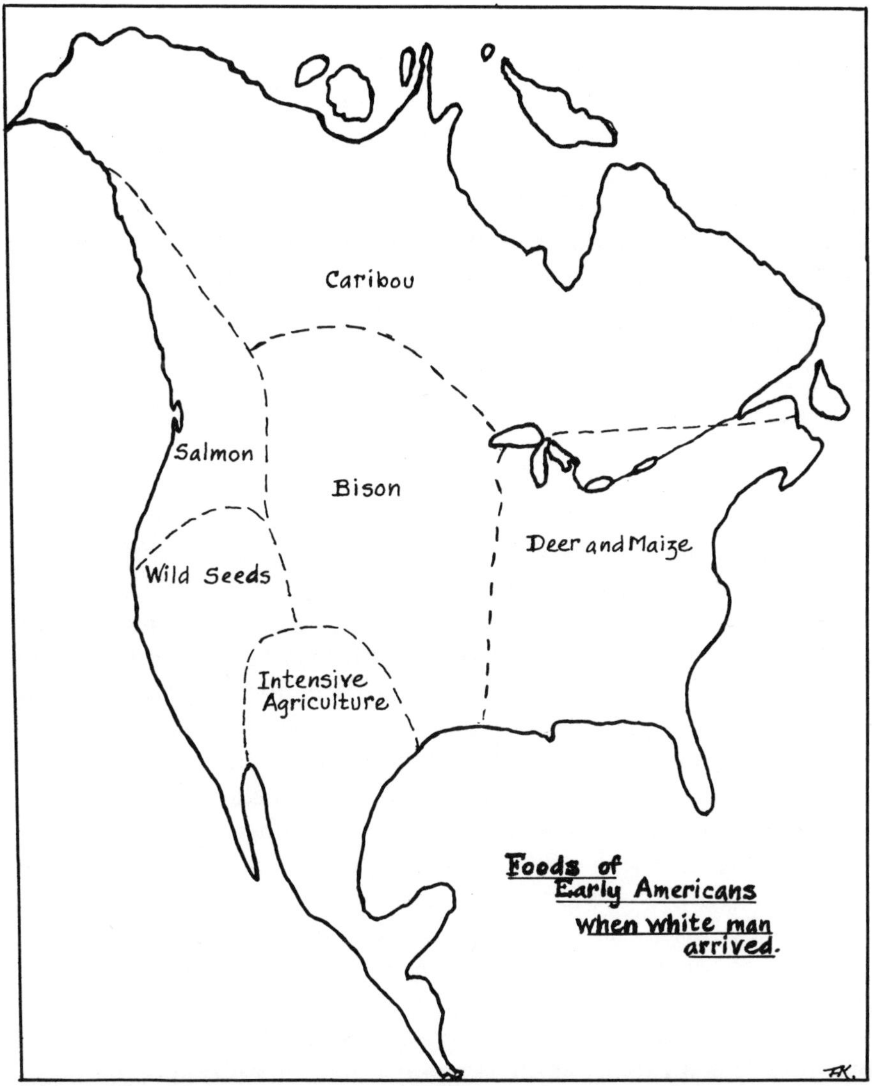
Caribou
Salmon
Bison
Deer and Maize
Wild Seeds
Intensive Agriculture
Foods of Early Americans when white man arrived.
F.K.

Indian gave them food, much they had never before seen—let alone eaten! Over the years Indian warriors taught the immigrants to thread their way over countless trails through the heavy forest, how to hunt and fish by methods unknown to whites, how to make and use Indian watercraft, and how to construct snowshoes and use them in waist-deep snow.

Indians also introduced white people to stone and copper tools, weapons, utensils, and implements and taught them how to fashion buckskin garments. They demonstrated to whites a way of life that was both endearing and secure. Through trade, Indians supplied furs and an abundance of necessities to whites in America and Europe—and revolutionized styles both here and abroad. Indian arts and crafts also influenced many aspects of artistic and intellectual life here. Even the gold and silver taken from Indians of the Americas in the sixteenth and seventeenth centuries changed Europe, permitting nations that took the precious metals to build powerful armies and navies. And Indian political and social concepts profoundly influenced the daily lives of white settlers.

A question that arose among early pioneers concerned the young of the tribes. Why did Indians have no problem with their children? When asked, they were unaware that children ever caused trouble. And—are you ready for this?—whites soon learned that Indians avoided overprotecting their young! Parents cherished a child's golden age of innocence, and they had traditional sets of precautions that kept children from resenting family or tribal orders. By the time a baby was six weeks old he was no trouble, tucked in a cradleboard propped against a tepee pole or resting on his mother's back, while she went about her daily work. When he began to crawl and investigate everything, including red hot coals in the tepee, no one yelled, "No! No!" The mother only watched that the flame didn't engulf him. "He must learn directly from the pain of the flame so he will let it alone," his mother said quietly as he jerked his tiny hand back. His anger was directed at the hot coals—plainly the source of the pain. He learned his lesson. He would avoid coals thereafter!

And much wisdom Indians possessed whites failed to recognize. Take this minister of the Gospel! When he reproached a chief with the immorality of his people, saying, "You don't even know which children around you are your own," this sympathetic reply came back; "I cannot understand you white people. You love only your own children. We love all children!" And this despite the fact that Indians did not mate with more than one of the opposite sex.

A human society without door locks can tolerate no thief—nor a troublesome individual if there is no jail. Yet, speaking to a band of Iroquois, a white pastor told them that he reminded his congregation regularly not to steal or murder. After the sermon an old Iroquois asked the preacher why Christians did those things. "No one ever steals or murders anyone within our tribe." When the pastor asked the chief's permission to place a missionary among the Iroquois, the chief was shocked. His reply? "Don't you think white poeple who steal and murder need the missionary more than we Indians?"

It was common knowledge that anyone who stole in the tribe, and this happened rarely, was chastised so severely that the person became an outcast. There is a moral here far beyond the cliché that dishonesty does not pay. Under such strict rules, Indians were oriented into tribal society at an early age. Youths' attention was directed to mastering the duties of adults and doing so without a tired, disinterested look! Theirs was a life of action—boys trained to become superior hunters and warriors, girls to master cooking, tan hides, sew, rear children, and make pottery.

Where were the American Indians when the United States entered World War II? Ready to fight for this country even though they already had lost it! Sioux rushed the recruiting stations. So did the Menominee, Chippewa, Winnebago, Sac, Fox, and others. The Indian regarded conscription a personal insult. "Since when," a new Indian recruit demanded, "has it been necessary to draft an Indian to fight?" Southern Cheyennes and Menominees let the world know that not one man of their tribes was drafted—everyone in war service volunteered. A Chippewa in Wisconsin, body mangled by an earlier injury, painfully moved himself along the highway in a wheelchair to the nearest recruiting station miles away and was saddened when refused the honor of joining the armed forces of the United States. In 1942, the marine corps perplexed Japanese codebreakers by putting Navajo Indians on the radio in their native tongue. And in battle overseas Indians gave a good account of themselves. They not only understood warfare but the teamwork and sacrifice necessary for victory.

A few Indians of the Southwest, about A.D. 1000, developed a miraculous etching process. Used was a weak acid, presumably made from fermented cactus juice. Designs were etched on seashells that came by trade from the Pacific Ocean. The practice ceased in about a century, due possibly to a single family's magic secret. Still, this may have been the first known etching anywhere in the world.

Prehistoric Indians had many languages. Some authorities claim there were about nine hundred Indian dialects when white people first came to America. So many different tongues could lead to total confusion and make a translator soon yell uncle. Fortunately, a few elderly members of a tribe could translate enough language of neighboring tribes so that one understood the other. Then, also, portions of the conversation were augmented by use of the good old Indian sign language. It has been said that the sign language of Plains Indians was the finest gesture language ever devised by man.

No unspoken tongue in world history compares in vocabularly and geographical scope with the Indian code of signs. Scientists believe it was used over all of North America, perhaps even into South America. The signs were a separate language, capable of expressing the most complicated idea or abstract thought. They could carry the longest story, as well as the most complex discussion.

Sign language, of course, is extremely old. Signs usually mimicked nature. *Fish*, for instance, is shown by a gliding, wiggling motion of the hand, *cold* by holding fists in front of the body and shivering. *Autumn* is a dropping of the fingers, like falling leaves. Some signs display wry humor. *Woman* is the motion of combing the hair; *quarrel* by holding up the index fingers and jerking them apart, repeated several times, mimics two persons springing at each other. *Hunger* is shown by a cutting sign at the stomach, *night* by making the sign for *world*, then quickly covering it up. The sign for *baby* is the rocking of the arms; *friend* is two fingers held together firmly.

Whether the same symbols were universal over North America is not known. Some signs surely varied between distant tribes, such as those of the eastern and western coasts. Nonetheless, most signs were so widely known that a Winnebago from Wisconsin could exchange thoughts with a Cheyenne from Wyoming or a Delaware

Fox squirrel: "Aren't them acorns good?"
Courtesy of the Wisconsin Department of Natural Resources.

from the eastern seaboard even though a few signs differed to a degree. The meaning of new signs was so obvious they could be interpreted without difficulty, and to imagine this communication between Indian tribes of North America occurred at a time when white man's "civilized" England had so many dialects a farmer from Somersetshire could not make himself understood by a farmer from Yorkshire—150 miles away.

American Indians contributed generously to the esthetic life of whites. Although basketry and pottery were some crafts in which they excelled, beading was their very own—at least in its original form. The most distinguished beadwork in the world at the time was that of our Indians—no other people produced anything like it. Most Indian tribes had beads of crude form, but artful beadwork was a unique technique devised by the Great Lakes, Prairies, Plains, and Southwest Indians.

Pottery making was not one of the early arts practiced by primitive people. In fact, it was unknown to those who migrated from Asia to North America. Nomads simply did not turn to pottery making, because such utensils were too fragile to move from place to place. After they lived for longer periods at established locations, they hit upon the idea of manufacturing a container from clay which, when fired, could be used for an endless variety of domestic purposes.

Ceramic art may have been an accidental outgrowth of basketry. Sedentary life encouraged its development, and soon it came into its own as a special field of expression. Interestingly, pottery making began independently in different places of the world—about 7,000 years ago in the Near East, some 4,500 years ago in China, and perhaps 3,000 years ago in North America.

Pottery is a sensitive indicator of transformations within a civilization. Made and decorated by hand, it is a flowing record of changes at a given location that reflect trends from century to century. By studying pots or portions thereof along with other artifacts, the archaeologist can reconstruct history of a race that left no written record.

In prehistoric times, like today, making oneself amount to something through art was a masterful accomplishment. And it was the women who made most of the pottery and decorated it. Through the pot an artist's concept of life was recorded as she saw it, portraying the simple glories of the present and what little was known of the distant past. Champions of the art were the pottery makers who lived in the quiet pueblos of our Southwest a few hundred years ago—applying pleasing colors, eloquent shapes, and artful designs to their pots. Tribes with no great warriors, nor renowned hunters, nor history-making statesmen oftentimes excelled as artistic pottery makers—and no fine art, perhaps, was more original than that of the early potter. No art also was more in tune with one's imagination. Beautiful was the product, even though the potter had no wheel on which to rotate the pot while it was formed, nor fancy kiln in which to dry it. Yet, under the most primitive methods, an artful and durable pot was manufactured.

The prehistoric Indian seldom if ever smoked just to be smoking. He smoked with some degree of flourish at special occasions, civil or religious ceremonials, or when sealing an agreement between tribes. When doing so, the pipe was passed from one individual to another—sometimes only from one chief to another. A

Courtesy of the Capitol Times, Madison, Wisconsin.

"Who-o-o?! Me?"

puff from the pipe sealed the verbal agreement, just as white men today affix their signatures to a document indicating approval. A chief placing an X on a United States government treaty meant nothing to him. Only if the parties had smoked a peace pipe would the agreement be sealed. If this was not done, there was no agreement. And women never smoked!

How surprising that many nutritional foods Indians used were indigestible, even poisonous, in their natural state. Such foods required careful processing before they were eaten. One example is the oak acorn, normally unpalatable before proper preparation. Early nomads of prairies and forest used acorns from twenty-seven species of oaks. Acorns have nutritive qualities, having been eaten by at least half of the Indian tribes. But acorns contain bitter tannic acid in varying amounts and all or most of it must be removed. To process them, the meats first were removed from the shells, then pulverized in a mortar and taken to a stream for the leaching procedure. Placed in a depression in the sand prepared for the purpose, water was slowly passed over or poured through the acorn meal. This leeching process was repeated until the bitter taste of tannic acid disappeared. Then the meal was ready for cooking.

Potatoes were a staple food of many tribes. They were boiled or baked among coals. The use of potatoes as a food dates back some six thousand years, when Indian women in the valleys of the Andes Mountains on the Pacific coast of South America cultivated them. Even prior to this date, Indians learned that the tubers of the wild potato plant were safe to eat. The plant belongs to the nightshade family, and the berries born above ground are poisonous. But the skill of these ancient Indian women in developing better and more nourishing plants from wild potatoes, maize, beans, rice, tomatoes, and others kept their families healthy and strong.

Europeans did not know the bean before they arrived here, yet Indians from Chile to Canada grew many varieties, including kidney, navy, lima, and scarlet. The tomato also was new to whites, yet the Indians in Central America grew it thousands of years before white settlers arrived. Also, American Indians some six thousand years ago recognized the strange, armored fruit of the pineapple as edible. As time progressed, these various plants were accepted by tribe after tribe—at least a few thousand years before white men reached our shores.

But maize was the most important food Indians gave white people. Tests on core samples taken from the soil in Mexico City revealed wild maize pollen eighty thousand years old—long before the Asiatic nomads reached the American continent. But Indians developed the plant and cultivated it so that it spread from tribe to tribe—north, south, east, and west—until it became the king of plant foods among many tribes of Central, North, and South America.

Students of the subject today well understand that Indians gave abundantly to the people of this world. Let us consider one specific contribution—food. It is almost unbelievable that half of the crops grown worldwide today were developed and domesticated by American Indians; thus white people knew these foods only after they arrived here. Two of these, corn and potatoes, are two of four foods most important in the world today.

More than eighty known plants domesticated by Indians were introduced to white people. Included are such staple foods as tomatoes, squashes, beans, peppers, peanuts, avocadoes, cacao (for chocolate), chicle (for chewing gum), nuts, pineapples, and a host of other items placed on our present-day table. And the Indian manioc, cultivated for its edible tuberous roots, has become a favorite food in African nations.

Even cotton, grown here and abroad today, was derived from plants domesticated by Indians of America. Rubber, first used here, has become a significant item in world commerce. Tobacco, first seen by Columbus as cigars in Cuba, has become a plant craved by people over the globe. More important to the human race than tobacco are some fifty drugs, including coca (for cocaine and novocaine), cinchona bark (the source of quinine), datura (a pain reliever), curare (a muscle relaxer), cascara sagrada (a laxative), and ephedra (a nasal remedy).

But the greatest individual Indian gift to white people was the fertile and mineral-rich land of North America. Though it may be considered a seizure rather than a gift, white settlers of America obtained with the land an endless variety of lakes, streams, forests, and wildlife. Best of all, the American Indian kept these resources in a condition unprecedented, compared to modern times. Though used for centuries, yes, for thousands of years—the boundless natural resources of the land remained virtually intact.

Yet that is not all! Indians contributed generously to our present way of life—designs for utilitarian articles, canoes, kayaks, snowshoes, dog sleds, toboggans, parkas, moccasins, hammocks, ponchos, smoking pipes, cigars, and rubber syringes. Given to white settlers was the recipe for making maple syrup and sugar. The rubber ball and the game of lacrosse are Indian innovations. Designs for many manufactured articles and goods—baskets to jewelry—followed Indian trends. Indian names identify several states, counties, cities, mountains, rivers, and lakes. And the English language has absorbed a variety of Indian words, including *chipmunk, oppossum, skunk, raccoon, woodchuck, moose, cougar, tobacco, hominy, pecan, hickory, tomato, squash, toboggan, tomahawk, canoe, kayak, tepee, wigwam,* and *papoose.* Adopted Indian expressions include "warpath," "bury the hatchet," "warpaint," "trail-tree," "paleface," "no-see-um" (a tiny insect with aspirations similar to those of a female mosquito), "Indian summer," "walking Indian file," and "Happy Hunting Ground."

Winnebago women have for centuries made colorful baskets from black ash wood.

Long ignored by whites, Indian culture finally has come into its own. Reviewed today are ancient Indian methods of raising and teaching their young, and white people want to know more about why Indian children were so well disciplined. During American colonial days, leaders recognized that policital organizations of some tribes were extraordinarily successful and that the League of the Iroquois was particularly outstanding. Benjamin Franklin was one who viewed the Iroquois government with great respect—so much so that he proposed adoption of some Indian methods into the union of American colonies. Consequently, the League of the Iroquois not only influenced the union of colonies indirectly, but set the direction for the new government being formed under the Constitution of the United States. Citing one instance, in compromising bills on which to act, House and Senate conferees adopted methods similar to those used by tribes within the League of the Iroquois.

Indians oftentimes displayed humor of such sober nature it went unrecognized by whites. And in later years, after association with whites, some youths became pranksters. Take the case of the tribe living on a bluff overlooking the Hudson River that was attempting to pattern its life after white settlers living nearby. One morning the chief, appearing strangely disheveled, called an emergency meeting for all boys of the tribe. "Now," he asked, "who pushed outhouse over cliff?" He recited the touching story about young George Washington who cut the down the cherry tree—the honesty of George who admitted the deed. "Now," the chief spoke again, "who push outhouse over cliff?" "I did!" the chief's own son quickly admitted and in return received a severe reprimand. "But father," the boy asked, "didn't George's father praise his son for his honesty when he admitted he cut the tree down?" "Son," demanded the chief, "his case different, 'cause George's father not in tree when tree fell!"

And there was the Indian of contemporary times who offered a story on conservation for the benefit of whites. Published in a farm journal was a picture of an abandoned farmhouse resting on a field heavily gullied. Offered was a cash award by the editor for the best story telling what happened. An Indian wrote this narrative and won the prize:

Picture show white man crazy. Build big tipi. Cut down trees. Plow hill. Water wash, soil gone. Buck gone. Everything gone: No bison. No grass. No maize.

Indian no plow land, keep trees. Trees make shade. Make bow and spear. Keep grass. Bison eat grass. Indian eat bison. Hide cover tipi. No hunt work. All time hunt. White man loco!

Our modern lives have been influenced by ancient Indians more than we care to admit, and usually every case is exquisitely understated. Our hunting techniques, our woodcraft skills, even our boy and girl scout organizations were inspired by the healthy outdoor life of Indians. Viewing the disappearance of our once great forests, the serious overcrowding of cities, the pollution of our air and water, and the explosion of our population, we look longingly at the life and habits of this disciplined race of prehistoric people to learn more fully where our present failures lie.

In his book *The Quiet Crises*, former secretary of interior Stewart L. Udall writes: "It is ironical that today the conservation movement finds itself turning back to ancient Indian land ideas, to the Indian understanding that we are not outside of nature, but a part of it. From this wisdom we can learn how to conserve the best parts of our continent. In recent decades we have slowly come back to some of the truths that the Indians knew from the beginning: that unborn generations have a claim to the land equal to our own; that men need to learn from nature, to keep an ear to the earth, and to replenish spirits by frequent contacts with animals and wild land. And most important of all, we are recovering a sense of reverence for the land." Instead of fiercely subduing nature, modern man, through utter necessity gradually is reverting to the Indian way of life and learning to live in harmony with the natural environment.

Did ancient Indians have a language? You can bet your new pair of moccasins they did, but not a written language in the truest sense. Still, they expressed themselves adequately with it. They also were masters of distinct and known hand movements that conveyed messages to those unfamiliar with their particular dialects. Art designs and picture diagrams on skin, wood, and horn conveyed quiet stories they wished to convey to viewers. And the age-old hieroglyphics on cliff walls tell something about the Indian everyday life.

Motion pictures and television programs today reflect the influence of the Indian on white man, but unfortunately too many of these interpretations of Indian history and culture are far from fact. Mythology and folklore, the unwritten literature of tribes, provide a rich heritage to our American way of life, although much ancient-Indian culture still remains ignored.

Rooted in antiquity, Indian folk tales dominated the lives of tribes. Intertwined with political, social, and religious habits and beliefs, the stories relayed approved rules of behavior. Hundreds of these folk tales, a resource as rich in mythology as those of ancient Greece and Rome, remain largely unrecognized today. But many tribes, even in this modern era, express folk-tale and religious beliefs in their ceremonial dances and sacred rituals.

Several non-Indians have used Indian themes. Take Longfellow's *Songs of Hiawatha* and Cadman's *From the Land of Sky Blue Waters*. So at long last, some white men recognize there is much to learn in studying the Indian way of life. And the Indian's reverence and understanding of the natural environment begins to reflect a fresh oasis in a nation made desert by blacktop and concrete, unlivable with noisey machines, and monotonous by people following a rushing schedule day after day. It has now been established that a certain quiet is essential for a person to lead a healthy life, and that a pleasing environment is required to make one's conscience at peace with itself.

Yes, contributions by ancient Indians to our way of life are profound indeed. They gave short, meaningful sentences. Their response to a question was direct and to the point, consistent with eloquence—much like that of a defense attorney today—no additional information was voluntarily given. And silence to an Indian was a moment at ease. With this choice bit of philosophy, they may have taught us more than we care to disclose.

White man's way of life was as mysterious as it was unreal to the American Indian. Why in heaven did white man kill off the bison, an animal with nourishing meat that fed and took care of itself on the range, and substitute domestic cattle instead—animals he had to feed and house? Such preposterous reasoning made no sense to the Indians!

Furthermore, the Indian did not agree with white man's personal ownership of land. Land belonged to the Great Spirit above—held in trust by a tribe for succeeding generations to use. No human could own land. When a tribe released land to the United States government, only the use of the land was given and only for a temporary period. When government payments to the tribe ended, the chiefs understood the land reverted back to them for their further use. Horses, food, and clothing—these material possessions could be individually owned, sold, or given. But land? Never!

The Indian point of view is fittingly expressed in a letter by Chief Sealth of the Duwanish tribe to Pres. Franklin Pierce in 1885. The chief lived at the time on land now included in the state of Washington.

> The Great Chief in Washington sends word that he wished to buy our land. How can you buy or sell the sky—the warmth of the land? The idea is strange to us. We do not own the freshness of the air or the sparkle of the water. How can you buy them from us? Every part of this earth is sacred to my people. Every shiny pine needle, every sandy shore, every mist in the dark woods, every clearing and humming insect is holy in the memory and experience of my people.
>
> We know that the white man does not understand our ways, for he is like a cut rose—soon withered! One portion of the land is the same to him as the next, for he is a stranger who comes in the night and takes from the land whatever he needs. The earth is not his brother but his enemy, and his children's birthright is forgotten.
>
> There is no quiet place in the white man's cities. No place to hear the leaves of spring or the rustle of insect wings. But perhaps because I am savage and do not understand, the clatter seems to insult the ears. And what is there to life if a man cannot hear the lovely cry of the whippoorwill or the arguments of the frogs around the pond at night.
>
> The whites, too, shall pass—perhaps sooner than other tribes. Continue to contaminate your bed, and you will one night suffocate in your own waste. When the bison are all slaughtered, the wild horses all tamed, the secret corners of the forest heavy with the scent of many men, and the views of the ripe hills blotted by talking wires. Where is the thicket? Gone. Where is the eagle? Gone. And what is it to say goodbye to the swift and the hunt, the end of living and the beginning of survival.

Fortunately we are beginning to look with growing interest at prehistoric Indians' zest for life, their dance and drama, their tribal social organizations, and the gracious courtesy between family and other members of the tribe.

Sang Lydia Sigourney, America's popular poet of the first half of the nineteenth century:

> Ye say that all have passed away,
>   The noble race and brave
> That their light canoes have vanished
>   From off the crested wave;
> That 'mid the forests where they roamed,
>   There rings no hunter's shout;
> But their name is on your waters,
>   Ye may not wash it out. . . .
> Ye say their cone-like cabins
>   That cluster o'er the vale,
> Have disappeared as withered leaves
>   Before the autumn gale:
> But their memory liveth on your hills. . . .

Grant that ancient Indians lacked a wealth of material things we possess. But by the same token there are possessions, customs, and bad manners we could better do without, and which the early Indian did not have. He had no efficient tools. He had no machines. His agriculture, though effective, was crude compared to modern times. He lacked our scientific knowledge. He was totally without world communication. Yet Indian life, even with all these deficiencies, overflowed with joy and contentment. And this abundance of happiness continued for hundreds, yes, thousands of years.

What happened to North America's natural environment after centuries of Indian use? It suffered little if any. Can our present civilization do equally well? We hear that modern America cannot long endure the continued reduction and destruction of its natural resources. Our last hope rests with public opinion, that it will force us to prevent this catastrophe; in these days however, this may be a dangerous assumption!

Epilogue

Discoveries of ancient and "lost" civilizations of the past make one speculate concerning the heritage our republic will expose to diggers of the future. Negate nuclear and other man-made explosions where direct hits destroy for unknown distances. Conversely, nature's volcanic eruptions may preserve rather than destroy evidence at a particular site.

Should we assume, as scholar Sir William Flinders Petrie says, that civilizations average 1,400 years before engulfed by enemies from away or by their own inadequacies? Just how long will present-day buildings stand without repair before disintegrating and the land again swallowed by nature? A hundred, two hundred, and, if one is generous, three hundred years?

Bricks in time return to clay powder, and steel succumbs to the clandestine corrosion of concrete. Airborne gases, with destructive motives, penetrate structures. After a civilization disappears, perhaps a thousand years pass before a new people capture the site, perhaps covered with natural grass and forest. And this may be buried as much as ten feet below the original. Remember the fate of the Mayas—a superior culture for the time that reached its peak circa A.D. 1000? In fewer than eight hundred years after its collapse, virtually their entire civilization, along with their supercity Chicken-Itza of more than one hundred thousand inhabitants, disappeared!

Ironically enough, an archaeologist of the new people becomes involved. By persistent effort and detective instinct, he locates a cemetery underground with granite markers. Wind-blown soil over centuries buried it. Digging deeper, he discovers some gold and silver jewelry and gold from human teeth. During his digging, surprisingly, he also finds a fluted stone spearhead of ancient people who lived on the land perhaps eight thousand years before. Examining the granite markers, he finds unfamiliar writing. Persistent effort by schoalrs extracts the messages. They represent the lost civilization of the United States of America. Dates indentified are 1891, 2082, and 2197.

But then another archaeologist probing into the distant past discovers a rare find—a city dump nearby covered heavily with soil. He sifts the debris for bits of ancient knowledge in an attempt to learn what made the nation tick. No paper documents, no concrete, not even iron remains as the metal disintegrated. Choice discoveries are pieces of glassware, although soil chemistry made them iridescent. There are broken bottles—milk, cola, beer—with writing within the glass, mostly illegible. Remember the perfume and face cream bottles and jars of ancient Assyria and Egypt? These miniature cosmetic caskets used for self-beautification relayed a message about the life of these people of many centuries earlier.

So let us pray that the wise men and women of A.D. 4000 or 4400 or 4900, later or earlier, whichever it may be, are charitable in judging our present achievements, knowing they have so little on which to base their judgment. We also hope they find something worthwhile that we accomplished that may help them to improve their culture. Furthermore, we trust they will understand that we too judged in our own way the civilization on this continent before us and found notable achievements, especially in development of fruits, vegetables, and natural plant fibers new to us, and they left us a beautiful, unpolluted land.

For untold centuries people of one civilization studied ancients before them. Knowledge was gained and lost, and this evolutionary process we presume will persist as long as planet earth remains much as our Lord made it. Is there no end to time?

Appendixes

Appendix A

Finding Indian Relics Today

Have you had the urge to head for the country, find a spot where you believe an Indian camp once stood, walk the field looking on the ground surface until exhausted, then suddenly be rewarded by finding and holding in your hand a flaked point fashioned by ancient man a thousand years before the birth of Christ? Most of us have this impulse. Knowing that Indians flaked and used stone points for thousands of years, one can readily understand that not all relics of that ancient civilization have been discovered. By applying ingenuity and effort, many relics are yet to be found. Let no one convince you that all Indian artifacts lost in a hunt, in battle, and in camp have been picked up. Spearheads, arrowheads, and other artifacts fashioned by our American Indians are lying on the ground surface in fields. Any boy, girl, man, or woman can find these relics today, but . . .

First, one must know how to locate long-gone Indian campsites and hunting grounds. For time unknown, long before the horse of today was brought to America, Indians of the forest hunted deer more often than any other animal. Its meat, hide, horns, almost every part, contributed to their survival. And how did ancient Indian hunt deer? He still hunted carefully through their haunts at dusk, when the deer left their day beds in deep recesses and came out to feed in the more open woods. Setting himself at one spot, rarely did the Indian roam the woods in search of game. The Indian let game come to him. In the forest he selected a location along a game trail, one leading to a lake or stream, and waited.

En route to this location the lone warrior walked stealthily over dry leaves and twigs, his moccasioned feet scarcely making more noise than the wind rustling through the treetops. Stationing himself near water, the warrior sat down on an old log just off the trail,

Beckoned by the evening, Mr. Raccoon knows that it is time to awaken.

camouflaging himself with leafy branches. Selecting a location where wind blew his human scent away from the place the deer came to drink, he waited. He also used a primitive subterfuge, placing on his buckskin garment a few drops of deer musk gland concoction substantially stronger than his human scent. Its identifying odor a deer would readily recognize. Across knees lay his bow, with arrowshaft end set across the bowstring.

Within this leafy camouflage the Indian sat motionless, his buckskin clothing blending with the forest background. Birds, scolding excitedly when he came, soon settled down and moved freely again. A fox squirrel sitting on an overhanging limb above him calmly chattered. Chipmunks again darted around, ignoring the warrior sitting motionless.

Into this tranquil setting a buck cautiously followed the game trail, his hooves making no audible sound. Sniffing the air for scent of the dreaded puma or pack of timber wolves, he stopped for a moment, then unsuspectingly walked to the lake's edge. Still on guard, the buck stood for an instant, watching for any movement and listening for the excited calls of birds—calls warning of danger. Sensing no enemy, he quickly lowed his head to drink.

Until this very moment, the hunter made not a single move. As the deer drank, the warrior slowly, very slowly, raised the bow. Still camouflaged, he gently pulled back the bowstring to the limit, letting the arrow fly. The arrow pierced the buck's heart. Then the hunter froze. Leaping upward, the deer again landed on its feet. Standing motionless, the animal raised its antlered head, not knowing what caused the sudden pain. Seeing no enemy, the buck took a few steps and again stood still, but not for long, Soon he fell on his side—and there no longer was movement or life.

So look for Indian artifacts in fields near water. For protection from wild fires in the Midwest, for instance, Indians usually encamped on the north and east sides of streams inasmuch as prevailing winds during the dry season came from the south and west. Become saturated with confidence like the person who sees a glass of water half full while another sees it half empty. Finds will be more frequent if you can recognize the stone points at a glance, when they are partially covered with soil. Attempting to differentiate between arrowheads, spearheads, and knives while in the field is a waste of time. Points up to an inch and a half long usually are arrowheads. Those longer and thicker may be spearheads or knives.

If points are purchased, especially when acquired from unknown sources, do suspect fakes. Many of these are made from colored glass or a stone that flakes easily. Ancient North American Indians had no colored glass. It arrived after traders bartered colored glass for beaver skins. But ancient Indians did have volcanic glass, obsidian. Glass breaks easily; thus obsidian points oftentimes are found broken. An unbroken obsidian arrowhead or spearhead picked up in a field today is a rare find.

Hunting for Indian relics is a challenging hobby. Yet to some this may be as exciting as lying on one's stomach and watching dandelions grow. Spring is preferable—when fields are cultivated and rains frequent—and a hunter is less likely to miss seeing the points if forced to concentrate on a small area. But never should one sink a spade into Indian mounds, as these are graves or religious

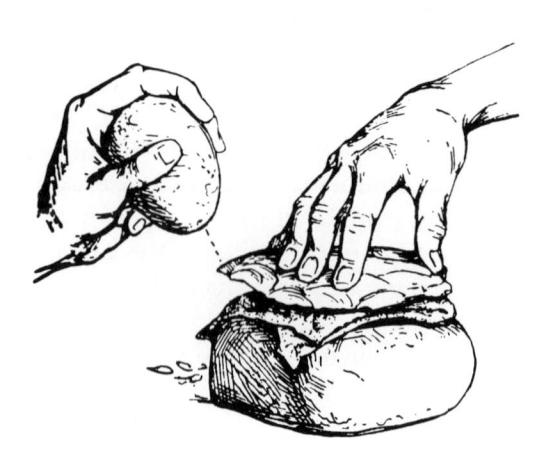

Courtesy of the Milwaukee Public Museum.

The preliminary shaping of a stone artifact, utilizing a hammerstone to flake the rock.

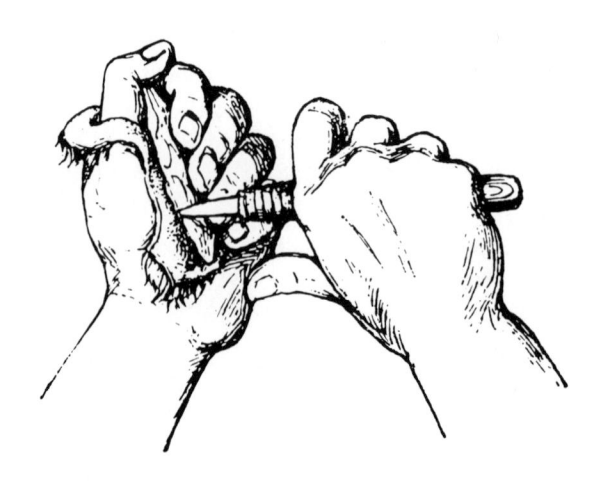

Additional shaping was done by applying pressure with the tip of an antler.

earthworks. And several states have laws that forbid raiding them. Professional archaeologists who represent public institutions, through permits, can dig into a few, but only to further scientific knowledge. Private artifact collectors must confine relic hunting to soil surface finds.

By following this procedure one can be adequately rewarded, and the author can bear witness to this fact. With a little ingenuity and big effort you may become surprisingly successful.

So find a likely site—one where you had not previously enjoyed the pleasure of intimate acquaintance. And finding a few relics may hypnotize a person with hunting fever. The marvelous capacity of finding oftentime leads to more looking and more finds.

Do request permission from the landowner if you wish to look for Indian relics on the individual's property. This is just common courtesy! Bring your best manner with you. When coming by motor vehicle, ask to park the machine in the farmyard; then the owner will know when you leave. You may be watched during your first visit. Always close gates when passing from one field to another. If no gates are located, roll under the bottom wire of the fence rather than crawl between wires. The reason for this is obvious—a broken wire, a damaged fence, and possible injury. Never smoke on someone's property. Tell them you will not do so when asking permission to hunt relics. Should a grass or woods fire develop, the owner will know you were not responsible. And treat the property as you would your very own!

Let us assume that you have found what appears to be an old Indian campsite location and one you want to explore. Examine the site carefully. Treat it with the reverence accorded wildlife species! Let it whisper to you. Listen for the ghosts of yesterday and the moccasined feet that walked there. Where were the huts located? Not in wet lowland, surely! They were located on the higher well-drained soil. Check that portion of the plowed field for lost or boken points and for pieces of broken pottery. Look for flakes where the stone points were struck. Walk the site systematically, examining the ground surface at an angle. Avoid looking straight down, because an arrowhead or other artifact seldom lies flat on the ground. Learn to recognize each when only a small portion is visible. Examine every flaked stone. You may be surprised what you find.

Grass or trees may have covered the campsite when Indians lived there. Sites wooded at that time may have little vegetation today, so examine sand blowouts carefully, especially those along watercourses. Indians oftentime chose sandy, well-drained sites for camps. They no more cared for mud around their dwellings than we do today.

Now! Do you think you can find some Indian relics? Just remember that you can if you think you can. Exhibit confidence like the small boy who informed his father he had just sold their mongrel dog for fifty thousand dollars. "For cash?" asked the father. "Practially," was the proud reply. "I swapped him for two twenty-five thousand-dollar cats." When involved in the enjoyment of looking, keep on keeping on. After heavy rainstorms is best. Walk through mud if necessary, and enjoy it. Paraphrasing the old joke, "The opera ain't over 'til the fat lady sings," your Indian relic hunt isn't over until you find a point. And, finally you find an arrowhead! Though partially broken, still it is a stone point flaked by ancient man. Speculating, what collision broke the stone and rendered it useless so no Indian warrior considered it useful? In what year, as white man measures time, was it flaked? Did it bear the venom of battle, or was it destined for the hunt? Did the point tear through flesh of game, or flesh and blood of a human enemy? Is it a recent product, say only five hundred years old, or an ancient one?

From the diagrams in appendix B you may be able to answer a few of these questions, i.e., its approximate age and the culture of the people at the time the point was flaked. Size and shape tell much of the story!

Appendix B

Identifying Stone Indian Artifacts

Spearhead Shape	Name	Culture	Age	Length
	Sandia Extremely Rare	Early Paleo-Indian	16,000 to 25,000 yrs. Perhaps older	2 to 4 inches Rarely longer
	Clovis Extremely Rare	Early Paleo-Indian	12,000 to 15,000 yrs. Possibly older	2 to 4 inches Average 3 inches
	Folsom Rare	Early Paleo-Indian	10,000 to 12,000 yrs. Perhaps older	1½ to 3 inches Average 2 inches
	Type and Culture 1. Early archaic 2. Archaic and woodland		2,000 to 7,000 yrs.	1-1/2 to 3 inches
	End Scrapper with Graver	Paleo-Indian and Archaic	Same age usually, as associated artifacts	1/2 to 2 inches

Projectile Points	Type	Culture	Age (Approximate)	Size
	Eared	Archaic	2,000 to 7,000 yrs.	1 to 4 inches
	Tapered Stem	Archaic	2,000 to 7,000 yrs.	Large and Small
	Side Notched	Archaic and Woodland	1,500 to 6,000 yrs	2 to 3 inches
	Long-eared	Archaic	2,000 to 7,000 yrs.	1 to 3 inches Occasionally Longer
	Small-stemmed	Archaic and Woodland	1,000 to 6,000 yrs.	Less than 1 1/2 inches
	Corner-notched	Usually Woodland	300 to 2,000 yrs.	Large and Small
	Small Triangular	Archaic and Woodland	300 to 5,000 yrs.	1 to 2 inches
	Large Triangular	Woodland	300 to 1,500 yrs.	3 inches
	Leaf	Woodland	300 to 1,500 yrs.	1 to 3 inches

Type	Culture	Age	Size
Knife	Early and Late Archaic through Woodland	2,000 to 7,000 yrs. Perhaps older	2 to 6 inches long
Flake knives	Paleo-Indian through Woodland	500 to 12,000 yrs. Perhaps older	1/2 to 2 inches
Gravers	Paleo-Indian	8,000 to 12,000 yrs. Perhaps older	Up to 2 inches long
Eared Drill	Archaic through Woodland	2,000 to 7,000 yrs.	2 to 4 inches long
Grooved Axe	Late Archaic and Woodland	300 to 5,000 yrs.	3 to 10 inches long
Celt or Ungrooved Axe	Archaic and Woodland	300 to 6,000 yrs.	2 to 10 inches long

Now—you found some Indian relics! Do keep a permanent record of the geographic location where each artifact was found.

Small artifacts should not be left lying around the home. Too often they are unknowingly discarded or they simply disappear. It is best to arrange them neatly in glass-covered mounts with all pieces found at one site mounted together. Large artifacts like axes and hammerstones, with essential information thereon, can be exhibited on shelves of a glass-front cabinet.

One striking fact about Indian relics today is that they remain conservatively abundant. When a site with artifacts is discovered, a collector will walk the same field year after year, seldom failing to find pieces worth preserving. Oftentimes one finds good productive sites in other fields nearby. Not only do Indian weapons of chase occur in some quantity, but objects of personal use and ornaments also.

How can such an abundance of Indian artifacts be explained? Through losses mostly, over a period of thousands of years. Then also, primitive people, like some persons today, had certain superstitions. Some Indians would not use an article previously owned by one who had died, least the "spirit" resent it. Thus the piece, no matter how beautiful and useful, was buried with the individual or discarded. Also, persons who consider their time and labor of little value, or who have no personal property other than bare necessities, oftentimes are careless with the few articles they do possess. Many prize specimens surely were lost in battle when a warrior had his life to worry about rather than the thought of losing arrows or spear. Articles also were unintentionally discarded with home refuse, or left behind when the village was attacked by an enemy and destroyed. Pieces oftentimes then became buried under a natural accummulation of soil dust and vegetation for hundreds, yes, for thousands of years.

Superstition also played a role in weapon loss. An arrow which killed an especially large bison, or a spear that felled a charging bear—these were highly prized while others which failed their owners were thrown away for punishment.

A certain element of mystery surrounds making a stone artifact. Fashioning an arrowhead in camp from a blank disc an Indian had buried in his private cache to keep the stone "soft" was accomplished with comparative ease. But when the warrior was on the trail and needed arrowheads, how was the task performed? This is how a Great Plains warrior flaked a point while Dr. J. F. Snyder, a white man, watched; published in "The Antiquarian," dated September, 1879.

> ... He then searched in the running water (of the creek) for something that he soon picked out, proving to be a fragment of vitreous quartz. Seating himself on a boulder near me, his next move was to unfasten and unwrap the sinew thread from the end of the arrowshaft and detach and remove the piece of stone arrow-head remaining in it, for it had broken when it struck the rocky ground. He placed the thread of sinew in his mouth to soften it and render it pliable. Then holding the quartz splinter on its edge with his left hand, on a smooth boulder as an anvil, with a small trap pebble as a hammer, he gently tapped the stone, first one edge, then on the other, striking off a tiny chip at each stroke until he soon had it reduced approximately to the dimensions he required. He had before seating himself, removed his quiver from his shoulder, and at this stage untied from its strap a buckskin string that suspended the point of a deer's horn, seven or eight inches in length, notched or grooved at its small end in a peculiar manner that I had not before noticed. The savage saw that I was intensely interested in his work and executed every movement deliberately and plainly in my view, as though he felt pride in his knowledge of the stone art. Now spreading the broad tail flap of his quiver in the palm of his left hand, with its inner or dressed side up, he placed upon it the quartz splinter he had blocked out, and held it firmly in place with the two smaller fingers of the hand clasped over it. With the point of his horn punch he then, by firm and careful pressure, broke from the edges flake after flake from the point of the embryo arrowhead along to its base. Stopping a moment to inspect the stone, he would reverse it and repeat the cautious pressing on the outer edge until directly its outline was that of the ordinary leaf-shaped, flint implement. He now reversed his deer-horn punch, when I noticed that it was ground at its upper or large end, to an obtuse or diamond point at one side, somewhat like that of a woodcarver's burin. Applying this stout point, by the same mode of pressure as before, to each side of the broad end of the stone alternately, the stone now resting for solid support on the heavy muscles at the base of the thumb, he soon chipped out the indented, lateral notches, defining the shank of

the arrow-head, which was now finished as completely, and perfectly proportioned, as any I ever saw. Fitting it in the cleft of the arrow-shaft, he took the slender thong from his mouth and soon had the new weapon securely fastened, his horn-punch tied to its place again, and, gathering up his quiver and bow, quickly vanished from view.

The whole process, from his selection of the stone adapted for his purpose, to the last tuck of the sinew strand in adjusting the finished implement to its shaft, did not exceed twenty-five minutes of time.

This chapter is directed chiefly to the amateur archeologist who looks for artifacts on the ground surface rather than the professional who digs up history by removing layer after layer of soil at one location. But there is history in ground surface finds also, infinite amounts of history, if it is recognized and recorded. It is the history of ancient Indians, a people who sounded no trumpet to call attention to their greatness. Their culture is becoming more and more recognized, though only a minute portion is documented and published. And white man's disrespect for these early Indians is imbedded in the conscience of this nation.

"What is Past is Prologue" are wise words of Shakespeare carved on the stone wall at the entrance to the beautiful Archives Building at our national capital. "Study the Past," carved on the opposite wall, are words equally significant. Although this proclamation refers to our nation's brief history, it applies well to the entire span of human life on earth. Thus, knowledge and lessons of the past help us to better understand the present, and are essential to guide our future.

Bibliography

Voluminous literature of Indians as told by explorers, traders, colonists, and historians prevails and is strikingly comprehensive. And it was written about these native Americans before the full impact of European ways began to change them. Later, studies based on field, laboratory, and research came from archaeologists, anthropologists, and other specialists. Over the years many works have appeared, with some but not all tending to become outdated soon by new findings of research and further study. Research papers and comprehensive studies have increased, and volumes of commendable works ranging from prehistoric cultures to Indian-white relations are available.

This bibliography is directed primarily to those works chiefly of interest and assistance to the nonspecialist. But much of the material may guide the more inquiring reader to intimate studies of individual tribes and to the various aspects of Indian life. For when we ignore the heroic past of the American Indians and neglect to include their great contributions to our own history, we weaken our very heritage.

Mention is being made of the many museums and libraries and national, state, and local historical societies that contain significant collections, sometimes including unpublished articles and manuscripts on American Indians. Some of these institutions are listed herewith:

Alaska Historical Library and Museum, Juneau
American Antiquarian Society, Worcester, Massachusetts
American Museum of Natural History, New York
American Philosophical Society, Philadelphia
Archives of Ontario, Toronto
Arkansas State Museum, State College, Arkansas
Arizona Pioneers Historical Society, Tucson
Arizona State Museum, Tucson
Brooklyn Museum, Brooklyn, New York
California Historical Society, San Francisco

Chicago Historical Society, Chicago
Chicago Natural History Museum, Chicago
Denver Museum of Natural History, Denver
Detroit Public Library, Detroit
Glenbow Foundation, Calgary, Alberta
Hudson's Bay Company, London and Winnipeg
Idaho State Historical Society, Boise
Illinois State Historical Society, Springfield
Indiana Historical Society, Indianapolis
Kansas State Historical Society, Topeka
Kentucky Historical Society, Frankfort
Library of Congress, Washington, D.C.
Los Angeles County Museum, Los Angeles
Maine Historical Society, Portland
Manitoba Historical Society, Winnipeg
Maryland Historical Society, Baltimore
Massachusetts Historical Society, Boston
Michigan (State) Historical Commission, Lansing
Michigan State Library, Lansing
Milwaukee Public Museum, Milwaukee
Minnesota Historical Society, Saint Paul
Missouri Historical Society, Saint Louis
Montana Historical Society, Helena
Museum of New Mexico, Santa Fe
Museum of Northern Arizona, Flagstaff
Museum of the American Indian, Heye Foundation, New York
National Museum of Canada, Ottawa
Nebraska State Historical Society, Lincoln
New Hampshire Historical Society, Concord
New Jersey Historical Society, Newark
New Mexico State Library, Santa Fe
New York Historical Society, New York
New York Public Library, New York
New York State Museum, Albany
Newberry Library, Chicago
Ohio Historical Society, Columbus
Oklahoma Historical Society, Oklahoma City
Oregon Historical Society, Portland
Peabody Museum of Archeology and Ethnology, Harvard University
Provincial Archives of British Columbia, Victoria
Provincial Museum, Victoria
Public Archives of Canada, Ottawa
Royal Ontario Museum, Toronto
Sheldon Jackson Museum, Sitka, Alaska
State Historical Society of Colorado, Denver
State Historical Society of Iowa, Des Moines
State Historical Society of Missouri, Columbia
State Historical Society of Montana, Helena
State Historical Society of North Dakota, Bismarck
State Historical Society of Pennsylvania, Philadelphia

State Historical Society of Wisconsin, Madison
South Dakota State Historical Museum, Pierre
Southwest Museum, Los Angeles
Tennessee State Library and Archives, Nashville
Texas Memorial Museum, University of Texas, Austin
Thomas Gilcrease Institute of American History and Art, Tulsa, Oklahoma
University of Arizona, Arizona State Museum, Tucson
U.S. National Archives and Records Service, Washington, D.C.
U.S. Smithsonian Institution, Washington, D.C.
Utah State Historical Society, Salt Lake City
Vermont Historical Society, Montpelier
Virginia Historical Society, Richmond
Washington State Historical Society, Tacoma
Wyoming (State) Archives and Historical Department, Cheyenne
Yale University Library, New Haven, Connecticut

The following is not intended to be a complete list of publications on Indians. It includes only important works that proved most helpful in the preparation of this book.

Amesden, Charles A. *Some Popular Misconceptions about Primitive Peoples and Their Study*. Vol. 6, no. 2. Los Angeles: Masterkey, 1932.
———. *Navaho Weaving*. Santa Ana, California; 1934.
Anderson, Edgar. "The Maize Collections from Painted Cave." In E.W. Haury, *Painted Cave, Northeastern Arizona*. Pub. No. 3. Dragoon, Arizona: Amerind Foundation, Inc., 1945.
Antevs, Ernst. *The Last Glaciation*. Research Series, No. 17. New York: American Geographical Society, 1928.
———. *The Occurrence of Flints and Extinct Animals in Pluvial Deposits near Clovis, New Mexico, Part II: Age of the Clovis Lake Clays*. Proceedings of the Academy of Natural Sciences of Philadelphia 87, 1935 a.
———. *Climate and Early Man in North America*. Edited by G.G. Mac Curdy. Philadelphia and New York, 1937.
———. "Correlation of Wisconsin Glacial Maxima." *American Journal of Science* 243-A (Daly Vol.), 1945.
Austin, H. Russell. *The Wisconsin Story*. Milwaukee, 1948.
Baerreis, D.A., Hiroshi Daifuku, and J.E. Lunsted. "The Burial Complex of the Reigh Site, Winnebago County, Wisconsin." *Wisconsin Archeologist* 35, no. 1 (1954).
———. "Chieftainship Among the Potawatomi: An Exploration of Ethnohistoric Methodology." *Wisconsin Archeologist* 54, no. 3 (1973).
Baerreis, D.A., and Reid A. Bryson. "Climatic Episodes and the Dating of the Mississippian Cultures." *Wisconsin Archeologist* 46, no. 4 (1965).
Baerreis, D.A., and Joan E. Freeman. "Late Woodland Pottery in Wisconsin as Seen from Aztalan." *Wisconsin Archeologist* 39, no. 1 (1958).
Baer, J.L. "A Preliminary Report on the So-called Bannerstones." *American Anthropologist* 23 (1921).
Bailey, Tom. *The Comanche Wars*. Derby, Connecticut, 1963.

Barrett, S.A. "Ancient Aztalan." *Bulletin of the Public Museum of the City of Milwaukee* 23 (1933).
Beard, Charles A. and Mary R. *The Basic History of the United States.* New York 1944.
Bell, E.H. (ed.). *Chapters in Nebraska Archeology. Vol. 1.* Lincoln: University of Nebraska, 1936.
Bennett, J.W. *Archeological Explorations in Jo Daviess County, Illinois.* University of Chicago Publications in Anthropology, Archaeological Series. Chicago: University of Chicago Press, 1945.
―――. "Archeological Horizons in the Southern Illinois Region." *American Antiquity* 10, no. 1 (1944).
Berthrong, Donald J. *The Southern Cheyennes.* Norman, Oklahoma: University of Oklahoma Press, 1975.
Berry, Brewton, and Carl Chapman. "An Oneota Site in Missouri." *American Antiquity*, no. 3 (1942).
Black, G.A. "Excavation of the Nowlin Mound." *Indiana Historical Society Bulletin* 13, no. 7 (1936).
Bluhm, Elaine, and David J. Wenner, Jr. "Prehistoric Culture of Chicago Area Uncovered." *Chicago Natural History Museum Bulletin* 27, no. 2 (1956).
Brandon, William. *Book of Indians.* New York, 1961.
Bretz, J. Harlen. "The Stages of Lake Chicago: Their Causes and Correlations. *American Journal of Science* 249, no. 6 (1951).
Broecker, W.S., and J.L. Kulp. "Lamont C14 Studies." *Bulletin of the Geological Society of America.* 66, no. 12, part 2 (1955).
Brown, John Mason. *Daniel Boone: The Coming of the Wilderness.* New York: Random House, Inc., 1952.
Campbell, E. W. C., et al. *The Archeology of Pleistocene Lake Mohave.* Southwest Museum Papers, No. 11, Los Angeles, 1937.
Campbell, William H. and Elizabeth W. *The Pinto Basin Site.* Southwest Museum Papers, No. 9, Los Angeles, 1935.
Carter, G. F. "Archeological Notes on a Midden of Point Sal." *American Antiquity* 6 (1941).
Clark, W. P. *The Indian Sign Language.* Philadelphia.
Cole, Fay-Cooper, and Thorne Deuel. *Rediscovering Illinois.* University of Chicago Publications in Anthropology, Archeological Series. Chicago: University of Chicago Press, 1937.
Collier, Donald, A.E. Hudson, and Arlo Ford. *Archeology of the Upper Columbia Region.* Vol. 9, no. 1. University of Washington Publications in Anthropology. Seattle: University of Washington Press, 1942.
Collins, H.B., Jr. *Outline of Eskimo Prehistory, Essays in Historical Anthropology of North America.* Smithsonian Miscellaneous Collections, Vol. C. Washington, D.C., 1940.
―――. *Eskimo Archeology and Its Bearing on the Problem of Man's Antiquity in America.* Proceedings of the American Philosophical Society 86, no. 2 (1943).
Colton, H.S. *Prehistoric Culture Units and Their Relationships in Northern Arizona.* Museum of Northern Arizona, Bulletin 17, Flagstaff, Arizona, 1939.
Colton, H.S., and L.L. Hargrave. *Handbook of Northern Arizona Pottery Wares.* Museum of Northern Arizona, Bulletin 11, Flagstaff, Arizona, 1937.
Cooper, L.R. "The Red Cedar Variant of the Wisconsin Hopewell Culture." *Bulletin of the Public Museum of the City of Milwaukee* 16, no. 2 (1933).

Cooper, Paul. "Report of Explorations: The Archeological Exploration of 1938 by the Nebraska State Historical Society." *Nebraska History* 20, no. 2, 1939.
Crane, H.R. "University of Michigan Radiocarbon Dates I." *Science* 124, no. 3224 (1956).
Crane, H.R., and James B. Griffin. "University of Michigan Radiocarbon Dates II." *Science* 127, no. 3306 (1958).
Cunningham, Wilbur M. *A Study of the Glacial Kame Culture in Michigan, Ohio, and Indiana*. Occasional contributions from the Museum of Anthropology of the University of Michigan, no. 12. Ann Arbor: University of Michigan Press, 1948.
Curtis, Edward S. *The North American Indian*. Vols 4 and 5. Cambridge, Massachusetts; 1911. Vol. 6. Norwood, Massachusetts, 1926.
Cutler, F. S. *The Lady in the Lake*. Saint Paul.
Day, Donald. *The Hunting and Exploring Adventures of Theodore Roosevelt*. New York.
DeLand, Charles E. *The Aborigines of South Dakota. Part II: The Mandan Indians*. South Dakota Historical Collections, Vol. 4, 1908.
Dellinger, S.C., and S.D. Dickinson. *Pottery from the Ozark Bluff Shelters*. South Dakota Historical Collections, Vol. 7, no. 3, 1947.
Denhardt, Robert. *The Horse of the Americas*. Norman, Oklahoma: University of Oklahoma Press, 1975.
Deuel, Thorne. "Hopewellian Dress in Illinois." In *Archeology of The Eastern United States*, edited by James B. Griffin. Chicago, 1952.
Dillon, Richard. *Meriwether Lewis*. New York, 1965.
Dixon, Joseph K. *The Vanishing Race*. New York, 1913.
Dixon, R.B. "Some Aspects of North American Archeology." *American Anthropologist* 15, no. 4 (1913).
Dodge, Richard Irving. *The Plains of the Great West*. New York, 1877.
Dorsey, J. Owen, and Paul Radin. *Winnebago: Handbook of American Indians North of Mexico*. Edited by F.W. Hodge. Bureau of American Ethnology Bulletin No. 30, Part II, Washington, D.C., 1912.
Dorsey, James Owen. *A Study of Siouan Cults*. U.S. Bureau of American Ethnology, Eleventh Annual Report, 1889–1890, Washington, D.C., 1894.
Douglas, A.E. "Checking the Date of Bluff Ruin, Forestdale: A Study in Technique." *Tree Ring Bulletin* 9, no. 2 (1942).
Driver, Harold E. *Indians of North America*. Chicago: University of Chicago Press, 1961.
Elson, John A. "Lake Agassiz and the Mankato-Valders Problem." *Science* 126, no. 3281 (1957).
Embee, Edwin, R. *Indians of the Americas*. New York: Macmillan, 1939.
Farnham, Thomas Jefferson. *Travels in the Great Western Prairies*. Poughkeepsie, New York, 1841.
Fenton, William N. "Problems Arising from the Historic Northeastern Position of the Iroquois." In *Essays in Historical Anthropology of North America*, Smithsonian Miscellaneous Collections 100, Washington, D.C., 1940.
Fewkes, J.W. *Designs of Prehistoric Hopi Pottery*. Bureau of American Ethnology, Thirty-third Annual Report, Washington, D.C., 1919.
Figgins, J.D. "The Antiquity of Man in America." *Natural History* 27, no. 3 (1927).
Fletcher, Alice A. *Indian Ceremonies*. Salem, Massachusetts, 1884.
Foreman, Grant. *Pioneer Days in the Early Southwest*. Cleveland, 1926.

Fowke, Gerald. *Stone Art.* Bureau of American Ethnology, Thirteenth Annual Report, Washington, D.C., 1896.

———. "Material for Aborginal Stone Implements." *Wisconsin Archaeologist* 2, no. 10 (1894).

Fowler, Melvin L., and Robert L. Hall. *Archeological Phases at Cahokia.* Illinois State Museum Research Series, Papers in Anthropology, No. 1, 1972.

Fox, George R. "A MacGregor Bay Cemetery." *Wisconsin Archeologist* 10, no. 2 (1930).

Frazer, Robert W. *Forts of the West.* Wayne, New Jersey: Norman Publishing Co., 1975.

Gibson, Edmond P. "Ancient Mounds near Grand Rapids in the Lower Grand River Valley and in Southwestern Michigan." *Michigan Archaeological Society News* 1, no. 3 (1954).

Gifford, E.W. *Pottery Making in the Southwest.* University of California Publications in American Archaeology and Ethnology, Vol. 23, no. 8. Berkeley and Los Angeles: University of California Press, 1928.

Gilfillan, Joseph A. *The Ojibway.* New York:

Gilmore, M.R. *Arikara Uses of Clay and of Other Earth Products.* Museum of the American Indian, Heye Foundation, Indian Notes and Monographs, Vol. 2, no. 4, 1925.

Gjessing, Gutorm. "Some Problems in Northeastern Archaeology." *American Antiquity* 14, no. 4. (1948).

Gladwin, Harold S. and Winifred. *Some Southwestern Pottery Types.* Series I. Gila Pueblo, Medallion Papers, no. 8, Globe, Arizona, 1930.

Goddard, P.E. *Indians of the Northwest Coast,* 2nd ed. American Museum of Natural History Handbook Series, no. 10, New York, 1934.

Greenman, Emerson, F. *Michigan Mounds with Special Reference to Two in Missaukee County.* Papers of the Michigan Academy of Science, Arts, and Letters 7, Ann Arbor, 1927.

———. "Department of Archaeology." *Museum Echoes* 4, no. 8, 1931.

———."Review of *Sixty Years of Ontario Archeology,* by Kenneth E. Kidd, and *The Archeology of the Upper Great Lakes Area,* George I. Quimby." *American Antiquity* 19, no. 2 (1953).

Griffin, J.B., and R.G. Morgan, eds. "Contributions to the Archaelogy of the Illinois River Valley." *American Philosophical Society Transactions,* no. 1 (1941).

Griffin, James, B. *The Fort Ancient Aspect: Its Cultural and Chronological Position in Mississippi Valley Archaelogy.* Ann Arbor: University of Michigan Press, 1943.

Grinnell, George Bird. *The Cheyenne Indians.* New Haven: Yale University Press, 1923.

Guthe, Carl E. *Pueblo Pottery Making: A Study at the Village of San Ildefonso.* Papers of the Phillips Academy, Southwestern Expedition, No. 2, New Haven, Connecticut, 1925.

Haag, W.G. "Early Horizons in the Southeast." *American Antiquity* 7, no. 3 (1842).

Hagan, William T. *The Sac and Fox Indians.* Wayne, New Jersey, 1958.

Haines, Francis. "The Northward Spread of Horses Among the Plains Indians." *American Anthropologist,* 40, no. 3 (1938).

Halsey, John R. "Gillen 9 (47-VE-177): An Archaic-Woodland Campsite in the Kickapoo River Valley." *Wisconsin Archeologist* 55, no. 3 (1974).

Harrington, M.R. "Catawba Potters and Their Work." *American Anthropologist* 10, no. 3 (1908).

Hatt, Robert T., et al. *Island Life: A Study of the Land Vertebrates of the Island of Eastern Lake Michigan.* Cranbrook Institute of Science Bulletin No. 27, Bloomfield Hills, Michigan, 1948.

Haury, E.W. *Painted Cave, Northeastern Arizona,* Pub. No. 3. Dragoon, Arizona: Amerind Foundation, 1945.

Hebard, Grace Raymond *Sacajawea.* Glendale, 1933.

Henry, Alexander. *Travel and Adventures in Canada and the Indian Territories between the Years 1760 and 1776.* Edited by James Bain. Toronto, 1921.

Hewitt, J. N. B. "Sauk." In *In Handbook of American Indians North of Mexico,* edited by F.W. Hodge, Bureau of American Ethnology Bulletin No. 30, part 2, Washington, D.C., 1912.

Hinsdale, Wilbert B. *Indian Mounds, West Twin Lake, Montmorency County, Michigan.* Papers of the Michigan Academy of Science, Arts, and Letters 10, Ann Arbor, 1929.

Hodge, Frederick W. *Handbook of American Indians North of Mexico.* Bureau of American Ethnology, Bulletin 30, New York, 1971.

Hoffman, Walter J. *The Menominee Indians.* Bureau of American Ethnology, Fourteenth Annual Report. Washington, D.C., 1893.

Hoijer, Harry, et al. *Linguistic Structures of Native America.* Viking Fund Publications in Anthropology, no. 6, New York, 1946.

Hornaday, William T. *The Extermination of the American Bison.* Report of the United States National Museum, Washington, D.C., 1887.

Hough, Jack L. *Pleistocene Chronology of the Great Lakes Region.* Final Report on Project NR-018-122, Office of Naval Research, University of Illinois, Urbana, Illinois, 1953.

Hruska, Robert. "The Riverside Site: A Late Archaic Manifestation in Michigan." *Wisconsin Archeologist* 48, no. 3 (1967).

James, George Wharton. *Learning from the Indians.* Philadelphia, 1907.

Jenks, Albert E. *Minnesota's Browns Valley Man and Associated Burial Artifacts.* Memoirs of the American Anthropological Association, no. 49, Menasha, Wisconsin, 1937.

Jennings, Jesse D. *Prehistory of North America.* New York: McGraw-Hill Book Company, 1968.

Josephy, Alvin M., Jr., ed. *The American Heritage Book of the Indians.* New York, 1961.

Keesing, Felix M. *The Menomini Indians of Wisconsin.* Memoirs of the American Philosophical Society, Vol. 10, Philadelphia, 1939.

Kehoe, Thomas F. "The Distribution and Implications of Fluted Points in Saskatchewan." *American Antiquity* 31, no. 4 (1966).

Kidd, Kenneth E. "Sixty Years of Ontario Archeology." *Archeology of the Eastern United States,* edited by J.B. Griffin. Chicago, 1952.

Kinietz, W. Vernon. *The Indians of the Western Great Lakes 1615-1760.* Occasional Contributions from the Museum of Anthropology of the University of Michigan, no. 10, Ann Arbor, 1940.

Kroeber, Alfred L. *Cultural and Natural Areas of Native North America.* University of California Publications in American Archaeology and Ethnology, Vol. 38. Berkeley: University of California Press, 1939.

———"The Arapaho." *Bulletin of the American* Museum of Natural History 18, parts 1 and 2 (1902).

Kroll, Harry Harrison, and Mildred Y. Payne. *Mounds in the Mist.* London, 1969.

La Farge, Oliver. *A Pictorial History of the American Indian.* New York: Crown Publications, Inc., 1956.
Lapham, L.A., Levi Blossom, and George G. Dousman. *Indians of Wisconsin.* Menomonee Falls, Wisconsin, 1870.
Laut, Agnes C. *The Fur Trade of America.* New York, 1921.
Lavender, David. *Bent's Fort.* New York, 1921.
———. *One Man's West.* New York, 1956.
Lawson, Publius V. "The Winnebago Tribe." *Wisconsin Archaeologist* 6, no. 3 (1907).
Lewis, Meriwether, and William Clark. *Journals of Lewis and Clark.* Edited by Bernard De Voto. Boston: Houghton Mifflin Co., 1953.
Libby, O.G. *Typical Villages of the Mandans, Arikara, and Hidatsa in the Missouri Valley, North Dakota.* Collections of the State Historical Society of North Dakota, Vol. 2, 1908.
Libby, Willard F. *Radiocarbon Dating.* Chicago, 1952.
Lowie, Robert H. *The Northern Shoshone.* Collections of the State Historical Society of North Dakota, Vol. 2, part 2, 1909.
Luttig, John C. *Journal of a Fur-Trading Expedition on the Upper Missouri, 1812–1813.* Edited by Stella M. Drum, Saint Louis.
MacAlpin, Archie. *A Census of Mastodon Remains in Michigan.* Papers of the Michigan Academy of Science, Arts, and Letters 25, Ann Arbor, 1940.
McCracken, Harold. *Portrait of the Old West.* New York, 1952.
———. *The Charles M. Russell Book.* Garden City, New York: Doubleday, 1957.
———. *Frederic Remington—Artist of the Old West.* Garden City, New York: Doubleday, 1966.
McKenney, Thomas H., and James Hall. *The Indian Tribes of North America.* Folio: Philadelphia, 1836–44. Octavo: Philadelphia, 1842–44. Reprint. Edited by F.W. Hodge. Edinburgh, 1933.
McKern, Will C. "The Neale and McClaughry Mound Groups." *Milwaukee Public Museum Bulletin* 3 (1928).
———. "First Settlers of Wisconsin." *Wisconsin Magazine of History* 26, no. 2 (1942).
———. *Preliminary Report on the Upper Mississippi Phase in Wisconsin.* Milwaukee Public Museum Bulletin 16, no. 2 (1945).
Martin, Paul S., George I. Quimby, and Donald Collierer. *Indians Before Columbus. Twenty Thousand Years of North American History Revealed by Archaeology,* Chicago: University of Chicago Press, 1947.
Mason, O.T. *North American Bows, Arrows, and Quivers.* Annual Report of the Smithsonian Institution for 1893, Washington, D.C., 1894.
———. *Aboriginal American Basketry.* Annual Report of the Smithsonian Institution for 1902, part II, Washington, D.C., 1904.
Mason, Ronald J. *Late Pleistocene Geochronology and the Paleo-Indian Penetration into the Lower Michigan Peninsula.* Anthropological Papers, no. 11. Ann Arbor: Museum of Anthropology, University of Michigan, 1958.
Mason, Ronald J., and Carol Irwin "An Eden-Scottsbluff Burial in Northeastern Wisconsin." *American Antiquity* 26, no. 1 (1960).
Mera, H.P. *Ceramic Clues to the Prehistory of North Central New Mexico.* Laboratory of Anthropology, Technical Series, Archaeological Survey, Bulletin 8, Santa Fe, New Mexico, 1935.

Mills, W.C. "Excavations of the Adena Mound." *Ohio Archaeological and Historical Quarterly* 10, no. 4, 1902.

———. "Exploration of the Mound City Group." *Ohio Archaeological and Historical Quarterly* 31, no. 3, 1927.

Mooney, James. *The Aboriginal Population of America North of Mexico.* Smithsonian Miscellaneous Collections 80, no. 7, 1928.

Mooney, James, and Cyrus Thomas. "Chippewa." In *Handbook of American Indians North of Mexico,* edited by F.W. Hodge. Bureau of American Ethnology Bulletin No. 30, part 1, Washington, D.C., 1912.

———. "Menominee." In *Handbook of American Indians North of Mexico,* edited by F.W. Hodge, Bureau of American Ethnology Bulletin No. 30, part 1, Washington, D.C., 1912.

Mooney, James, and Frank M. Olbrechts. *Sacred Formulas and Medicinal Prescriptions.* Bureau of American Ethnology, Bulletin 99, 1932.

Moore, C.B. "Sheet-Copper from the Mounds Is Not Necessarily of European Origin." *American Anthropologist* 5, no. 1 (1903).

———. "Antiquities of the St. Francis, White, and Black Rivers, Arkansas." *American Anthropologist* 14, parts 1 and 2 (1910).

Moorehead, W.K. *The Stone Age in North America.* 2 vols. Boston and New York, 1910.

Morris, Earl H. *The Aztez Ruin.* American Museum of Natural History, Anthropological Papers, vol. 26, 1928.

Mott, Mildred. "Relation of Historic Indian Tribes to Archaelogical Manifestations in Iowa." *Iowa Journal of History and Politics* 36, no. 3 (1938).

Nero, Robert. "Surface Indications of a Possible Early Archaic Camp-Site in Wisconsin." *Wisconsin Archeologist* 36, no. 4 (1955).

Neuberger, Richard L. *The Lewis and Clark Expedition.* New York: Random House, 1951.

Niblack, A.P. *The Coast Indians of Southern Alaska and Northern British Columbia.* Annual Report of the United States National Museum for 1888, Washington, D.C., 1890.

Orr, Kenneth G. "Field Report on Excavation of Indian Villages in the Vicinity of the Spiro Mound." *Oklahoma Prehistorian* 2, no. 11 (1939).

Oswalt, Wendell, H. *This Land Was Theirs: A Study of North American Indians.* New York: Wiley, 1966.

Packard, R.L. *Pre-Columbian Copper-Mining in North America.* Annual Report of the Smithsonian Institution for 1892, Washington, D.C., 1893.

Parkman, Frances, Jr. *California and Oregon Trail.* New York, 1849.

Peters, Gordon R. "A Reevaluation of Aztalan: Some Temporal and Casual Factors." *Wisconsin Archeologist* 57, no. 1, Wis. series.

Pond, A.W. *Primitive Methods of Working Stone Based on Experiments of Halvor L. Skavlem.* Logan Museum Bulletin, no. 2, part 1, Beloit, Wisconsin, 1930.

Pope, S.T. *A Study of Bows and Arrows.* University of California Publications in American Archaeology and Ethnology, Vol. 13, no. 9. Berkeley and Los Angeles: University of California Press, 1922.

Putnam, F.W. *Notes on the Copper Objects from North and South America contained in the Collections of the Peabody Museum.* Peabody Museum of American Archaeology and Ethnology, Fifteenth Annual Report, Vol. 3, no. 2, 1881.

Quimby, George Irving. *The Goodall Focus, an Analysis of Ten Hopewellian Com-*

ponents in Michigan and Indiana. Indiana Historical Society, Prehistory Research Series, vol. 9, no. 1, Indianapolis, 1941.

Quimby, George I., and Albert C. Spaulding. "The Old Copper Culture and the Keweenaw Waterway." Fieldiana Anthropology 36, no. 8 (1957).

———. "A Hopewell Tool for Decorating Pottery." American Antiquity 14 (1949).

———. "An Old Copper Site at Menominee, Michigan." Wisconsin Archeologist 38, no. 2 (1957).

———. Indian Life in the Upper Great Lakes. Chicago, 1960.

Radin, Paul. The Winnebago Tribe. Bureau of American Ethnology, Thirty-seventh Annual Report, Washington, D.C., 1923.

———. The Winnebago Tribe. Lincoln: University of Nebraska Press, 1970.

Report of the Commissioner of Indian Affairs, Senate Executive Document No. 1, 24th Congress, 1st Session, 1835, and 2nd Session, 1836; Senate Executive Document No. 1, 25th Congress, 2nd Session, 1837, and 3rd Session, 1838.

Report of the Secretary of War, Senate Executive Document No. 1, 25th Congress, 3rd Session, 1838.

Reports of Explorations and Surveys to Ascertain the Most Practicable and Economcial Route for a Railroad from the Mississippi River to the Pacific Ocean, Washington, D.C. 1855.

Ridley, Frank. The Boys and Barril Sites. Publication No. 4 of the Ontario Archaeological Society, Toronto, 1958.

Ritchie, W. A. The Pre-Iroquois Occupations of New York State. Rochester Museum Memoir, no. 1, Rochester, New York, 1944.

Ritzenthaler, Robert E. Pre-historic Indians of Wisconsin. Milwaukee, 1967.

———. The Potawatomi Indians of Wisconsin." Milwaukee Public Museum Bulletin, 19, no. 3 (1953).

———. Some Carbon 14 Dates for the Wisconsin Old Copper Culture." Wisconsin Archeologist 39, no. 3 (1958).

———. "The Kouba Site: Paleo-Indians in Wisconsin." Wisconsin Archeologist, 47, no. 4, 1966.

———"A Cache of Paleo-Indian Gravers from the Kouba Site." Wisconsin Archeologist 48, no. 3 (1967).

———."A Probable Paleo-Indian Site in Wisconsin." American Antiquity (1967).

Ritzenthaler, Robert E., and Warren L. Wittry. "The Oconto Site—an Old Copper Manifestation." Wisconsin Archeologist 33, no. 4, (1952).

Ritzenthaler, Robert and Pat. The Woodland Indians of the Western Great Lakes, New York, 1970.

Roberts, Frank H.H., Jr. The Folsom Problem in American Archaeology. Annual Report of the Smithsonian Institution for 1938. Reprint of revised article from Early Man. Washington, D.C., 1939.

Robertson, Doane. A Comprehensive History of the Dakota or Sioux Indians. South Dakota Historical Collections, Vol. 2, 1904.

Ross, Marvin C. The West of Alfred Jacob Miller. The Walters Art Gallery, Norman, Oklahoma, 1951.

Rowe, Chandler, W. The Effigy Mound Culture of Wisconsin. Milwaukee Public Museum Publications in Anthropology, no. 3, 1956.

Ruxton, George Frederick. "Life in the Far West." Backwoods magazine (June November 1848).

Sandoz, Mari. Crazy Horse. Lincoln: University of Nebraska Press, 1961.

Sapir, Edward. Time Perspective in Aboriginal American Culture: A Study in

Method. Geological Survey of Canada, Anthropological Series, no. 13, Ottaw, 1916.

Sayles, E.B. *An Archaeological Survey of Texas*. Gila Pueblo, Medallion Papers, No. 17, Globe, Arizona, 1935.

Sayles, E.B., and Ernst Antevs. *The Cochise Culture*, Gila Pueblo, Medallion Papers, No. 29, Globe, Arizona, 1941.

Schultz, Gwen. *Glaciers and the Ice Age*. New York, 1963.

———. *Ice Age Lost*. Garden City, New York: Doubleday, 1974.

Sharp, R.P. "Shorelines of the Glacial Great Lakes in Cook County, Minnesota." *American Journal of Science* 251 (1953).

Sharpe, Philip B. *The Rifle in America*. New York, 1938.

Shetrone, H.C. *The Mound Builders*. New York, 1930.

Smith, Arthur, D. Howden. *John Jacob Astor*. Philadelphia, 1941.

Smith, Elmer, R. "Archaelogy of Deadman Cave, Utah" *Bulletin of the University of Utah*, 32, no. 4 (1841).

Smith, G.V. *The Use of Flint Blades to Work Pine Wood*. Annual Report of the Smithsonian Institution for 1891, Washington, D.C., 1893.

Smith, Winston, O. *The Sharps Rifle*. New York, 1943.

Spaulding, Albert C. "Northeastern Archaeology and General Trends in the Northern Forest Zone." In *Man in Northeastern North America*, edited by Frederick Johnson Andover, Massachusetts, 1940.

Spier, Leslie. *Ruins in the White Mountains, Arizona*. American Museum of Natural History, Anthropological Papers, Vol. 18, part 5, New York, 1919.

———. *Klamath Ethnography*. University of California Publications. In American Archaeology and Ethnology, Vol. 3. Berkeley and Los Angeles: University of California Press, 1930.

Spinden, H.J. *The Population of Ancient America*. Annual Report of the Smithsonian Institution for 1929, Washington, D.C. 1930.

Spooner, Harry L. "The Other End of the Great Sauk Trail." *Journal of the Illinois State Archeological Society* (1945).

Stafford, W. E. *Our Heritage from the American Indian*. Annual Report of the Smithsonian Institute for 1926, Washington, D.C., 1927.

Stallings, W.S., Jr. *Dating Prehistoric Ruins by Tree-Rings*. Laboratory of Anthropology, General Series, Bulletin 8, Santa Fe, New Mexico, 1939.

———. "A Basket Maker II Date from Cave du Pont, Utah. *Tree-Ring Bulletin* eight, no. 1 (1941).

Stanley, George M. "The Submerged Valley through Mackinac Straits." *Journal of Geology* 46 (1938).

———. "Minong Beaches and Water Planes in Lake Superior Basin." *Bulletin of the Geological Society of America* (1941).

Stephen, Decatur. "Alfred Jacob Miller: His Early Indian Scenes and Portraits." *American Collector (1911)*.

Stoltman, James B. "The Overhead Site (47 LC 20), An Orr Phase Site Near La Crosse, Wisconsin." *Wisconsin Archeologist* 54, no. 1 (1973).

———. "Two New Late Woodland Radiocarbon Dates from the Rosenbaum Rockshelter (47 DA 411) and Their Implications for Interpretation of Wisconsin Prehistory." *Wisconsin Archeologist* 57, no. 1 (1976).

Stoltman, James, B, and Karen Workman. "A Preliminary Study of Wisconsin Fluted Points." *Wisconsin Archeologist* 50, no. 4 (1969).

Stoutenburgh, John, Jr. *Dictionary of the American Indian*. New York, 1960.

Strong, W.D. *An Introduction to Nebraska Archaeology.* Smithsonian Miscellaneous Collections, Vol. 93, no. 10 (1935).
Swanton, J.R. *The Indian Tribes of North America.* Bureau of American Ethnology Bulletin No. 145, Washington, D.C., 1952.
Tax, Sol. "The Social Organization of the Fox Indians." In *Social Anthropology of North American Indians,* edited by Fred Eggan (Chicago, 1937).
Thruston, G. P. *The Antiquities of Tennessee.* Cincinnati, 1897.
Thwaites, F.T. "Pleistocene of Part of Northeastern Wisconsin." *Bulletin of the Geological Society of America* 54, no. 1 (1943).
Thwaites, F.T., and Kenneth Bertrand. "Pleistocene Geology of the Door Peninsula, Wisconsin: *Bulletin of the Geological Society of America* 68, no. 7 (1957).
Titterington, P.F. "Certain Bluff Mounds of Western Jersey County, Illinois." *American Antiquity* 1, no. 1 (1935).
Treholm, Virginia Cole, and Maurine Carley. *The Shoshonis, Sentinels of the Rockies.* Norman: University of Oklahoma Press, 1964.
Underhill, Ruth M. *Red Man's America: A History of Indians in the United States.* Chicago: University of Chicago, Press, 1953.
Vestal, Stanley. *Kit Carson.* Boston, 1928.
———. *Warpath.* Boston, 1933.
———. *The Old Santa Fe Trail.* Boston, 1939.
———. *Jim Bridger, Mountain Man: A Biography.* New York, 1946.
———. *Warpath and Council Fire.* New York, 1948.
———. *Joe Meek.* Caldwell, Idaho, 1952.
———.*Queen of Cowtowns: Dodge City.* New York, 1952.
———. *Sitting Bull, Champion of the Sioux.* Norman: University of Oklahoma Press, 1956.
———. *Happing Hunting Grounds.* Normal: University of Oklahoma Press 1975.
Watson, Don. *Cliff Palace: The Story of an Ancient City.* Ann Arbor: University Michigan Press, 1940.
Webb, C.H. "Stone Vessels from a Northeast Louisiana Site." *American Antiquity* 9, no. 4, 1944.
Webb, W.S., and W.D. Funkhouser. *Archaeological Survey of Kentucky.* University of Kentucky Reports in Anthropology and Archaeology, vol. 2, Lexington, 1932.
Webb, Walter Prescott. *The Great Plains.* Boston, 1931.
West, George A. *Copper: Its Mining and Use by the Aborigines of the Lake Superior Region.* Bulletin of the Public Museum of the City of Milwaukee, Vol. 10, No. 1, 1929.
———. "The Indian Authorship of Wisconsin Antiquities." *Wisconsin Archeologist* 6, no. 4 (1907).
———. *Exceptional Prehistoric Copper Implements.* Bulletin of the Public Museum of the City of Milwaukee, Vol. 10., no. 4, 1932.
Wheeler, Olin D. *The Trail of Lewis and Clark.* New York, 1904.
Whittlesey, Charles. *Ancient Mining on the Shores of Lake Superior.* Smithsonian Contributions to Knowledge, Vol. 13, no. 155, Washington, D.C., 1863.
Wilford, L.A. "A Tentative Classification of the Prehistoric Cultures of Minnesota." *American Antiquity* 6, no. 3 (1941).
Willoughby, C.C. "Primitive Metal Working." *American Anthropologist,* 5, no. 1, 1903.
Wilson, Curtis L., and M. Sayre. "A Brief Metallographic Study of Primitive Copper Work." *American Antiquity.* no. 2 (1935).

Wilson, Gilbert L., and Bella Weitzner. "The Hidatsa Earthlodge." *American Antiquity* 33, part 5 (1934).
Wilson, Thomas. *Arrowheads, Spearheads, and Knives of Prehistoric Times*. Annual Report of the United States National Museum for 1897, Washington, D.C., 1899.
Wintemberg, W.J. "The Sidey-Mackay Village Site." *American Antiquity* 11, no. 3 (1946).
Wissler, Clark, *The Relation of Nature to Man in Aboriginal America*. New York, 1926.
———. *The American Indian*. New York, 1931.
———. *Indian Beadwork*. New York, 1931.
———. *The Indians of the United States*. New York, 1940.
Wittry, Warren L. "A Preliminary Study of the Old Copper Complex." *Wisconsin Archeologist* 32, no. 1 (1951).
———. The "Raddatz Rockshelter SK 5 Wisconsin." *Wisconsin Archeologist* 40, no. 2 (1959).
Wittry, W.L., and R.E. Ritzenthaler. "The Old Copper Complex: An Archaic Manifestation in Wisconsin." *American Antiquity* 21, no. 3 (1956).
Wormington, H.M. *Ancient Man in North America*. Denver Museum of Natural History Popular Series, No. 4, 1959.
Wormington, H.M., and Robert H. Lister. *Archaeological Investigations on the Uncompahgre Plateau in West Central Colorado*. Denver Museum of Natural History Proceedings, No. 2, 1956.
Wray, Donald E. "Archeology of the Illinois Valley: 1950." In *Archeology of the Eastern United States*, edited by James B. Griffin (Chicago, 1952).
Yanovsky, Elias. *Food Plants of the North American Indians*, Department of Agriculture, Miscellaneous Publication No. 237, Washington, D.C., 1930.
Young, Stanley P., and Edward A. Goldman. *The Wolves of North America*. Washington, D.C., 1944.